IT'S ALL THE SAME

STOP LOOKING FOR THE SECRET AND BE YOUR OWN GURU

IT'S ALL THE SAME

STOP LOOKING FOR THE SECRET AND BE YOUR OWN GURU

DAVID ALLRED

ethos
collective

Printed in the United States of America

Published by Ethos Collective™
PO Box 43, Powell, OH 43065
www.ethoscollective.vip

LCCN: 2023922324
Paperback ISBN: 978-1-63680-241-1
Hardcover ISBN: 978-1-63680-242-8
e-book ISBN: 978-1-63680-243-5

Available in paperback, hardcover, and e-book

All Scripture quotations, unless otherwise indicated, are taken from the Holy Bible, New International Version®, NIV®. Copyright © 1973, 1978, 1984 by Biblica, Inc.™ Used by permission of Zondervan. All rights reserved worldwide.

Any Internet addresses (websites, blogs, etc.) and telephone numbers printed in this book are offered as a resource. They are not intended in any way to be or imply an endorsement by Ethos Collective™, nor does Ethos Collective™ vouch for the content of these sites and numbers for the life of this book.

Some names and identifying details have been changed to protect the privacy of individuals.

CONTENTS

INTRODUCTION

THIS COULD BE THE LAST SELF-HELP BOOK YOU EVER NEED

Faith in oneself is the best and safest course.

—Michelangelo

When you look at a rock, you probably just see a rock. If you're a geologist, you may see a specific type of material or formation, but still, it's just a rock. That's how Michelangelo's masterpiece *David* began. What we know as one of the greatest accomplishments of the Renaissance started as a huge chunk of expensive, uninspiring stone marred by imperfections.

Those imperfections convinced several experienced artists that the marble block was unusable. Believing nothing worthwhile or valuable could come out of that rock, they didn't want to waste the time and tremendous effort it would require to create *David* only to have the rock crumble mid-project or worse, after they'd completed the sculpture.

Michelangelo ultimately proved everyone wrong.

In September of 1501, twenty-six-year-old Michelangelo began to chip away at *David*. Unlike the artists who had abandoned their commissions or declined them altogether, he embraced the project with wholehearted passion. Wielding his chisels day and night for more than two years in the open courtyard of the Cathedral of Florence, Michelangelo worked rain or shine, sometimes skipping meals and sleep. He refused to allow anyone to see the sculpture until he revealed the masterpiece to the church council's members in January of 1504.

The perfection of Michelangelo's creation blew them away. The council members unanimously agreed that the sculpture was too exquisite to be put in the originally planned location atop the cathedral, so far from the people who wanted to admire it. Besides, the seventeen-foot-tall, six-ton statue was too massive to hoist up there anyway.

Working together, the church and city councils found a home for *David* in the Piazza della Signoria, the political center of Florence. Standing confidently in the heart of the city, with a defiant stare aimed at the giant of Rome, *David* became a symbol of freedom—and it propelled Michelangelo into fame. And, contrary to the originally commissioned artists' fears, the sculpture, which was later moved to its current home in Florence's Accademia Gallery museum, never crumbled. *David* remains one of the most well-known and treasured pieces of Renaissance art.

Right about now, you may be thinking, That's interesting, but this is a personal development book. What's up with the art history lesson?

I'm so glad you asked.

Let's look at a few parallels between what it took to create *David* and what it will take for you to become the person you want to be:

Michelangelo chipped away at an unformed hunk of marble to reveal what lay within all along. There may be some days or seasons of your life when you feel like an unfinished project. Unformed. Incomplete. Not good enough and certainly not a masterpiece. But just as Michelangelo found *David* within that rock, you already have what it takes to be the best version of yourself. That ability and power are within you, not *out there*. *David* wasn't pieced together. Michelangelo removed the excess to find the masterpiece within.

Michelangelo believed it was possible to create something new and beautiful with what he had to work with. The artist took on a project others had abandoned. Believing that "every block of stone has a statue inside it and it is the task of the sculptor to discover it," he worked around and with the imperfections in the stone rather than giving up on it.[1] Belief is perhaps the most critical element to your success. Belief in yourself and your capability to grow and create the life you desire changes the way you look at yourself and your place in the world. Without that persistent belief, the temptation to give up and accept the status quo can feel overwhelming.

Michelangelo worked with passion and purpose to reveal something awe-inspiring. But make no mistake; it was work. You've probably heard the misquoted, light-hearted quip supposedly from Michelangelo about his process that sounds something like, *It is easy. You just chip away the stone that doesn't look like David.* In reality, Michelangelo never claimed it was easy. On the contrary, he said, "If people

---

[1] https://www.michelangelo.org/michelangelo-quotes.jsp.

knew how hard I worked to get my mastery, it wouldn't seem so wonderful at all."

It is so easy to watch the montage of others' accomplishments and falsely assume that growth and change happen magically. One quick workout, one magic pill, one right decision or lucky break, and *BAM!* Life is perfect. In truth, nothing great happens without time, attention, and intention. *David* was inside that block of marble the whole time. Michelangelo was the one who was patient, determined, and focused enough to find him.

WHAT'S WAITING INSIDE YOU TO BE REVEALED?

I want you to think of yourself as *David.* You have something awe-inspiring waiting within you to be revealed. Your power, innate talent, ability, and potential are all waiting to be uncovered. And sure, you, like every other human on the planet, have some imperfect traits and circumstances that might complicate things along the way.

Here's the kicker: You are also Michelangelo. You are the only one who can work with and around those imperfections to reveal the greatness within you.

It took me years to understand the truth that I was the only one who had the answers for me.

I assumed everybody knew more about life and success than I did. I thought that if I was going to reach the next level, I needed a guru to show me the path and an expert to outline the keys to unlocking success and identify the pillars that would mark the way. Of course, I also needed a coach and a therapist to walk me through the steps so I could break through whatever roadblocks were holding me back.

The truth is, while many of the tools and strategies I've learned from coaches, counselors, and experts along the way have been helpful, they weren't the answer.

Was Tony Robbin's Date with Destiny an incredible, life-changing experience for me? You better believe it. Participating in that event is one of two of the best things I've done for my personal development. The other is working with a therapist. The hours I've spent talking with my therapist helped me better understand myself and what drives me. I consider that time and money well spent.

I don't regret the investment of energy and income I've put into learning from people like Tim Ferris, Wayne Dyer, Bo Eason, Dan Harris, Nick Ortner, Dan Sullivan, and so many other business leaders and personal development experts. I'll even share some of what I've picked up from them in the pages of this book.

Personal development—the guides, books, tools, courses, conferences, and workshops—has its place. It adds value to our lives. To a point.

The problem for self-identified self-improvement junkies like me is that we tend to glorify those personal development tools and strategies as "the thing" rather than seeing them as the vehicle that moves us toward the thing: the rich, full life we're seeking as we endeavor to become the best version of ourselves.

For years, I read the books, listened to the podcasts, and participated in self-help, personal development, and professional-growth courses, masterminds, and programs—each one offering the "secret" to success. Over time, I internalized the message that to be successful, I needed more information, a better plan, a more efficient system, and bigger, hairier, more audacious goals. I rationalized that if I felt stuck or dissatisfied in one area or another of my life, it was because I didn't have the right education, tools, or habits. The answer to that problem, of course, was to read another book or seek out another expert.

So I did. I read books. I studied. I attended workshops and conferences and seminars. I did everything I could to acquire more, newer, and better systems or secrets because I believed that was how I was finally going to break through the barriers that kept me from getting what I wanted out of life. Some of what I learned through those books, programs, and conferences has helped me become the person I am today. None of those things, however, provided *the* answer—the *secret*—to creating the life I wanted.

IT'S ALL THE SAME

My perspective shifted one day while I was talking with a friend over a bottle of wine.

I mean, it was a seismic activity kind of shift.

My friend shared that, from her point of view, most of the world's major religions are all the same. She surmised that Judaism, Christianity, Islam, Buddhism, and the rest shared similar goals, philosophies, and teachings. (You may have strong feelings about that one way or the other, but we're not going there in this book. I'm not here to change your religion, just your mindset.)

As she spoke, her points struck a chord for me, but the tones that resonated had nothing to do with religion and everything to do with my perpetual search for the secret to life. I reflected on all the personal development content I had consumed through the years. Sure, each speaker, author, coach, program, or system offered a few unique points, but one common thread ran through all of them. A thread that, if removed, would unravel every one.

The success of each strategy, tactic, or system relied on one thing: *me.*

I was the deciding factor that made any approach effective—or not.

In that moment of paradigm-shifting clarity, I realized that I was the one who held the chisel that would reveal my potential. No one else could do it for me. No one else was close enough to the problem (me) to uncover the solution (also me).

Like sculptors who gave up on bringing *David* out of that hunk of rock (or refused to try in the first place), no one else would ever be as dedicated to my success as I was.

I had to be as committed and creative as Michelangelo if I was ever going to achieve my true potential as David. Not *David* the sculpture, but David Allred—the real and best me I could be.

The same is true for you.

Consider this book your chisel. And like the other tools you've picked up on your search for success, you can use this chisel to reveal what's already within you.

This book isn't the secret to success. You are.

If you commit to that truth with wholehearted passion, you'll uncover the best version of yourself.

Let's get started.

1

WHO'S WRITING YOUR STORY?

It ain't what you don't know that gets you into trouble.
It's what you know for sure that just ain't so.

—Mark Twain

A funky pop-art image of a smile hangs in my office. To anyone else, the smile, complete with big teeth and bold braces, might seem like an odd choice for wall art. To me, however, that image represents a story from my past and a reminder for the present. Here's the backstory: The private school I attended as a child didn't have classes beyond intermediate grades, which meant I'd be starting middle school in a new school. Being the new kid in any school is hard. Being the new kid with crooked front teeth in a public middle school . . . well, no one wants to be that guy. I sure didn't, anyway, and I was the guy with the big, crooked front teeth. So, in the summer leading up to middle school, I asked my parents to schedule an orthodontist appointment for me.

The way my front teeth had decided to come in had made it apparent to everyone that I would need braces *someday*.

The problem was I came from a long line of procrastinators. Although my parents didn't dispute the inevitability of braces, they weren't too concerned with the timing. Someday would eventually come. I, on the other hand, was adamant that *someday* came before the first day of middle school. Weeks of pestering and reminding my parents to make an appointment went by without a trip to the orthodontist. Finally, I threatened to play hooky until I got braces. I meant it. I wasn't going to start school without braces. I knew the problem wouldn't be fixed before classes started, but my image—and my story— would be different. People would know that I wasn't oblivious to or ignoring the problem but was working to fix the problem. I didn't have the words for it back then, but I knew, even at twelve years old, I needed to advocate for myself. I needed to be the one who wrote my story. That funky art hanging in my office serves as my reminder to be that advocate today in my relationships, work, and life.

The opening line of any story is an invitation to learn—or stop listening. Whether that's with "Once upon a time . . ." or "You're not gonna believe this . . ." or "Back in my day . . . ," the beginning of a story matters. It's from that first line that the story takes shape. As a twelve-year-old, I didn't want the first line of my story to be about some kid with a grin that inspired bullies to attack.

What about you? How is the first line of your story impacting the way people see you? More importantly, how is the story you're telling *yourself* affecting the way *you* see you?

I'm going to let you in on a secret that many people don't understand: You are the narrator of your story. That means you get to decide how

YOU ARE THE NARRATOR OF YOUR STORY.

2

your story starts and how it progresses. Just like any good storyteller, you determine where to focus the attention and action of the narrative, which means the plot, theme, climax, and resolution are up to you.

Oh, I get that you may not feel like you're the one directing the scenes.

- You might be stuck living out the narrative someone gave you as a child: You're worthless. You'll never amount to anything. You're too (fill in the blank). You should be more like your brother or sister.

- Or maybe you feel frustrated because you believe you're at the mercy of your circumstances, and frankly, sometimes those circumstances stink. After all, your boss and the economy set the limits on your career potential and your income, right? Your health and habits are the results of your heredity and upbringing, and there's nothing you can do to change those things . . . or is there?

Chances are, your life's story isn't going the way you'd imagined it would. That's true for a lot of people. It was certainly true for me for quite a few years, which is how I know that if you want to change the story, you can. As Oprah said, "You have a right to change your mind."

If you're feeling frustrated with your life, I'm glad. Not because I want you to be unhappy, but because it's only when humans get tired of being stuck or living in a dissatisfying state of status quo that we stand up and say, "That's enough! There has to be more to life than this!" When you reach that point, you'll be ready to do whatever it takes to change your circumstances. You'll demand a plot twist and rewrite the narrative of your life in a way that is more interesting, enjoyable, and fulfilling.

I hope that's where you are today: ready for a new beginning. This is your story and you are the narrator, so it's time to take a more active role in your life.

If you could write a new story, what would it be? Guess what? You're writing your story now. Just by being here and reading this, you are changing your story. How do you want your life to be? What is it that is holding you back?

What Story Are You Telling Yourself?

You will succeed or fail based on the stories you tell yourself and others.

—Bo Eason

"Story is everything," says Bo Eason, author of *There's No Plan B for Your A-Game*. The former NFL player changed careers after enduring one too many surgeries. In the mid-2000s, he wrote and acted in his own play. Today, he aims, through his writing and speaking career, to help individuals, teams, and businesses discover and use their stories as a launching pad for success.

Why is knowing your story so important? "You can't live out your dream unless you understand your personal story on the most intimate level," Bo explains. "You must know what story you're telling yourself about yourself because that greatly influences the story you tell the world about yourself, and it determines the life you will live. It doesn't matter what you want to do. It only matters what story you tell yourself—and then how you live out that story every single day until you gain mastery."[2]

---

[2]   Bo Eason. "Who's Dictating Your Personal Story." BoEason.com. https://boeason.com/whos-dictating-your-personal-story.

Did you catch that? Your desire to do something isn't enough to overcome the story you believe about yourself.

> YOUR DESIRE TO DO SOMETHING ISN'T ENOUGH TO OVERCOME THE STORY YOU BELIEVE ABOUT YOURSELF.

The story Bo grew up hearing from his dad was that he and his five siblings were "the best." Every day, his dad woke them up by reminding them they had what it took to win. Bo believed that message and set his sights on being the best at whatever career he chose to pursue regardless of the obstacles—and there were plenty.

At this point, you might be thinking, *That's great for Bo, but my childhood was nothing like that . . . and things have only gone downhill from there.*

I don't know what the stats are, but my guess would be that too many people grow up with negative beliefs about themselves. Even if you had supportive and encouraging parents, there was probably a frustrated teacher, school bully, or an ex-boyfriend or girlfriend who may have tried to convince you that you were a failure in one aspect or another. Or maybe you tried to do something new or different and made a fool of yourself (or at least *felt* as if you'd made a fool of yourself), and the pain of that embarrassment has kept you from venturing too far off the safe and familiar path.

All of your experiences, including any number of traumatic events during childhood—an unwanted move, your parents' divorce, a prolonged illness, or the death of a loved one—shape the stories you tell yourself about your capabilities, potential, and even self-worth. It doesn't take a research study to see the connection between adverse childhood experiences and adult anxiety, depression, and family relationship issues (although there are plenty of studies to prove the correlation).

The more you repeat stories from your younger years, the more ingrained they become in your psyche. Eventually, those stories become part of who you are. They shape the way you think about yourself, and the way you think about yourself then determines the kind of person you are.

No one grows up without some sort of challenge, unwanted change, or trauma. So how is it that some people reach adulthood with an expectation of success while others leave the nest burdened with the baggage of pain and a dismal outlook on life? How can children from the same family who experience the same circumstances come to have polar opposite views of themselves, the world, and their place in it?

Part of the answer lies in the reality that every person is unique. We each experience life through our own perspective, which is colored by our attitude, personality, and mindset. The way we remember and tell our story—over and over again—and then live out that story is another factor in that equation. This is why, as Bo notes, we must be intimately aware of the stories we tell ourselves. That awareness, when paired with a deep understanding of self, opens the pages of our stories so we can rewrite the lines that don't serve us well.

One of Stephen Covey's seven habits of highly effective people is "Seek first to understand, then to be understood." In context, his advice is about trying to understand where other people are coming from before trying to get them to understand your own point of view. The strategy is about empathy and compassion, and it's an effective one for any relationship—including the relationship you have with yourself.

Think about it: When you screw up (because we all do), what is your first reaction? If you're like a lot of people, your knee-jerk response might be to berate yourself:

Why can't I do anything right?
I'll never get this.
Why do I even bother trying?
I'm so stupid.

IT'S ALL THE SAME

I'm just clumsy.
This is just the way I am. I can't change.

YOU'LL LIVE UP TO
YOUR EXPECTATIONS OF
YOURSELF—NO MATTER
HOW HIGH *OR LOW*
THEY ARE.

If those phrases sound familiar, I want you to consider the quote from Bo that opened this section: "You will succeed or fail based on the stories you tell yourself and others." You'll live up to your expectations of yourself—no matter how high *or low* they are.

Some people have grown so accustomed to negative, pessimistic, or even hateful self-talk that they don't think twice about it—it seems normal.

If that's true for you, stop and ask yourself, *would I say those things to someone I loved?*

Probably not. You wouldn't say such hurtful things to a stranger on the street, much less to your close friends, spouse or significant other, or child. So why say them to yourself?

If you think that self-talk doesn't matter, think again. Numerous research studies show that the way we talk to ourselves matters. Deeply. Your words, whether you say them aloud or only in your head, affect the way you deal with depression, handle disappointment, perform in sports, and so much more.

So, if you want to change your life, start by changing the way you speak to yourself—change the way you tell your story. Stop beating yourself up and start giving yourself a little more grace.

You screwed up? Great! What did you learn from the experience? What will you do differently next time? What did you do *right* this time that you need to do again?

Overwriting old narratives requires that you regularly repeat your new story to yourself—the story you *want* to live

7

by—and then follow through by living out that story. Start by having compassion for yourself. Forgive yourself if you need to, and give yourself credit where credit is due. Let your new story be one of possibility because the truth is, you already have what it takes to be the person you want to be.

What would it look like if you replaced whatever negative story you may have been telling yourself with a positive and encouraging line?

YOU ALREADY HAVE WHAT YOU NEED

Man is designed for accomplishment, engineered for success, and endowed with the seeds of greatness.

—Zig Ziglar

I've done a lot of things and enjoyed a decent amount of success, but I don't see myself as special. I'm just another person seeking to be the best version of myself. I've always wanted more for my life. I crave excitement and energy, fun and great friendships, bigger experiences, and greater success.

With those desires in mind, I spent years pursuing the best strategies for mental, physical, and professional success. You see, my old story was that I didn't have the right information, the right system, or the right skills. Bottom line: I thought being *me* wasn't enough. So, I purchased and participated in countless personal development programs. Without fail, each time the smoke from the special effects cleared and the heightened emotions settled, the same disheartening truth came to light: I was still me.

I was the same person after the event that I was before. Maybe I felt a little more inspired or a bit more optimistic about my future—for a while. But within a few days or a couple of weeks, the rush had worn off.

Daily life had taken its toll.

The mundane had crept back in.

And I hated it!

Maybe you can relate. If so, you probably have a collection of dogeared self-help and professional growth books. (Or maybe you've listened to the audiobooks so many times that you can repeat them verbatim.) You've probably purchased an array of digital courses and gone to at least a few conferences in hopes of changing your life for the better.

If you're hoping that you'll find an invitation to another seminar at the end of this book, I'm sorry to disappoint you. I don't have a course, coaching program, or conference to offer you (much to my publisher's dismay). Those things have their place and value, but it feels disingenuous to offer you the "secret" at a seminar when the whole point of this book is that you'll never find *your* secret *out there.* I don't have the secret to your life. *You do.*

After my prolonged search for the magical key that would open the door to my perfect life, I started to understand the futility of my efforts. The paradigm-altering conversation with my friends that I shared in the introduction shifted my focus from *out there* to *in here.* I started to look within for what I'd been missing. Somewhere along the way, I recalled a comment my uncle had made: "If you know enough to walk across the room and pick up a self-help book, you already know what you need." I brushed off his words initially, thinking they were too simplistic. I thought, *There wouldn't be a*

> KNOWING THAT YOU NEED OR WANT TO IMPROVE IS HALF THE BATTLE. OF THE REMAINING HALF, 10 PERCENT OR LESS IS ABOUT ADDING TO YOUR KNOWLEDGE. THE REST, AND THE MOST CRUCIAL PART, IS PUTTING WHAT YOU ALREADY KNOW INTO PRACTICE.

multi-billion-dollar self-help industry if all we had to know was that we needed to change. When I started to look inside myself for the answers, however, I understood my uncle's message. Knowing that you need or want to improve is half the battle. Of the remaining half, 10 percent or less is about adding to your knowledge. The rest, and the most crucial part, is putting what you already know into practice.

When I say that professional and personal development (PD) is "all the same," my intent isn't to disparage any program, course, or coach. I've learned from so many great people through the years. My guess is that you have too. This is probably *not* the first book in this genre that you've picked up. That's a good thing. Just as we become a product of our stories, we are (or can be) shaped by the knowledge we acquire. We can't unlearn what we've taken to heart. You can't *unring* the bell.

A while back, I heard Natalie Burt make a comment to that effect—we can't unlearn what we know—as she shared a story about the first time she heard Coach Michael Burt speak. You'll learn more about Coach Burt in a few pages, but suffice it to say he is a powerhouse of motivation and drive. Natalie and Michael are married now, but they weren't when she sat in the audience that first time, taking page after page of notes as he spoke.

What she learned that day blew her mind—and made her angry.

Natalie met with Coach Burt a few weeks after the seminar and showed him her notes. "No one had ever told me any of this," she said. "If anybody ever told me this, I would have lived my life differently." Coach Burt's response: "Ignorance can be cured. Stupid is forever." No longer ignorant and nowhere near stupid, Natalie put what she'd learned from Coach Burt into practice, and her life took a sharp upward turn.

You and I aren't ignorant. And we certainly aren't stupid. In fact, if you're anything like me, you've been collecting knowledge for a long time.

Acquiring knowledge is the easy part. It's fun! Beyond that, engaging in possibility thinking in safe, high-energy spaces can put us in a euphoric state. It's a temporary high, though. When the shine wears off, we crave more—another webinar, a new coach, the latest technique—and the cycle with its highs and lows continues.

On the surface, that desire seems pretty harmless, doesn't it? After all, what's so bad about self-improvement?

Absolutely nothing *if* you're actually improving and seeing real, lasting changes in your life. But as Tony Robbins says, "Knowledge is not power. Knowledge is only potential power. Action is power." If all you're doing is chasing the temporary high that comes with acquiring more information and ideas, you're going to come down with a crash when the realization hits that knowledge alone changes nothing.

Change requires engaging both the cognitive mind (the part that soaks up all that learning) and the conative mind (the part that pushes you into action). Most of us have gotten really good at the learning side of things. This is why I'm fairly confident you don't need another program, seminar, or guru to guide you to your version of success. It's far more likely that you need to **believe and act on the truth that you already have what you need.**

That's the story I hope you'll start telling yourself today. You already have the seeds of greatness inside you. They may be buried deep, but they are there. You just need to let them grow.

YOU ALREADY HAVE THE SEEDS OF GREATNESS INSIDE YOU. THEY MAY BE BURIED DEEP, BUT THEY ARE THERE. YOU JUST NEED TO LET THEM GROW.

Now that we're into this, is there something you recognize that you've gained, grown from, or changed as a result of stepping outside your comfort zone in the past? If you're like me, you have notebooks full of ideas. What's to stop you from picking one and putting it into action today?

HOW: GO AFTER IT!

An object at rest stays at rest unless acted upon by an outside source. You have to be that outside source.

—Michael Burt, author of Flip the Switch

At the end of each chapter, I'm including a "How" section because it bugs me when books offer motivation without application. Sometimes, we need help getting started. That said, I want you to read this section with an open mind—meaning open to all sorts of *hows*. What I'm sharing are approaches that have worked for me. If they resonate with you, too, great! Try out the ideas and strategies for yourself. But if you're already doing something that works for you, keep doing that! Implementation and action are far more important than modality.

Honestly, I almost didn't include the "How" sections because I didn't want you to get hung up on the modality—on doing the exact right thing and getting it perfect every time. For one thing, you're human, which means continuous perfection is an unrealistic goal. Sure, do your best. Always. But stop worrying about whether or not you're using the *right* system. There are so many paths you can take, and as long as you're moving toward the destination of your choosing, you'll eventually get there.

Think about it this way: If you want to improve your health, you could do Pilates or yoga. You could hop on your

Peloton or swim a few laps. Any type of exercise you *actually do* will raise your heart rate, help reduce stress, and burn calories. It's all the same.

Similarly, the goal of psychotherapy is to equip you to "learn how your own mind works. It allows you to navigate your feelings, build healthier habits, and change your mindset so that your life looks more like you want."[3] Psychologists and licensed therapists rely on a wide variety of theories and modalities, from cognitive-behavioral therapy to interpersonal or family therapy to art therapy and more. For decades, mental health professionals have debated which therapy is best or most effective, but study after study has found all legitimate forms of therapy to be beneficial. The practitioners and their approaches may be very different, but the consistent outcome of participating in therapy is the patient's improved mental health.

In ancient times, all roads led to Rome. Today, you can choose the destination and the route you want to take to get there. If being your best self is your focus *and* you put in the work consistently and persistently, you'll see improvement. Guaranteed. So don't hold off on putting in the effort. There's no magic course or coach that's going to *fix* you. Just find or develop a plan that motivates you, then get into motion—and don't stop until you arrive at your destination.

With that prefacing disclaimer out of the way, I want to close this section with a word on persistence. Because as Coach Michael Burt says, "Most people have dreams, but they don't have the persistence or intensity to pursue those

---

[3] "Science behind Therapy." Mental Health America. https://mhanational.org/science-behind-therapy

dreams, so they settle. They retract or retreat and just live an ordinary life."[4]

Coach Burt is a former championship women's basketball coach who is known today for his success as a life and business coach. Before he turned ten years old, he knew he wanted to be a coach when he grew up. Focused on that dream, he had a job as an assistant coach prior to his eighteenth birthday. As a self-professed disciple of Stephen Covey's teachings, he adhered to the Whole Person Paradigm with his players. Using that whole-person approach, Coach Burt steadily built a career helping others reach their greatest potential—beginning with his high school basketball players. His young players came together on the court, but basketball was sometimes the only thing they had in common. They came from different socioeconomic backgrounds with different family structures and challenges at home, and they possessed varying degrees of academic and athletic abilities. Believing that his job was to bring out the best in all of them, he sought to create not just a winning team but individuals who won at life.

That philosophy remains at the core of his coaching practice today. The way he brings out the best in people, he explains, is "to inner engineer people to produce at higher levels by speaking to and coaching their body (skill), mind (knowledge), heart (desire), and spirit (confidence)."[5] In other words, by coaching the whole person.

In his latest book, *Flip the Switch*, Coach Burt offers a strategy for activating what he calls the Prey Drive—the instinct we have to pursue what we want. It's innate, but, as he explains, "Unfortunately, most people have never found

---

[4] "Ep. 215 Activate Your Prey Drive with Michael Burt." *Reminder Media Podcast.* https://remindermedia.com/podcast/ep-215-activate-your-prey-drive-with-michael-burt.

[5] MichaelBurt.com. https://coachburt.com/about/5

it, or it's gone dormant. Or it needs to be reactivated on a pretty consistent basis. People start with good intentions but fail to follow through."[6]

Can you relate? I sure can! It's easy to start something. It's way harder to finish it well. So how do you maintain the energy to persist? Read on for a few ideas.

FIVE THINGS THAT ACTIVATE YOUR PREY DRIVE

The first step is to *activate* a desire that is strong enough to move you to action. Coach Burt identifies five main activators in *Flip the Switch*. They are things that get us moving. What works for you might not work for me, so you have to understand what's important to you.

Competition—Do you have a competitive spirit? Competition can be between you and a teammate or opponent, or it can be you versus you. If competition motivates you, then throw down a challenge!

Fear of Loss—What will you lose if you don't succeed at your goal? The fear of losing money, prestige, comfort, security, or relationships can be a powerful motivator.

Environment—Does your environment inspire you? Or does it drag you down? How can you set up your surroundings to keep you focused?

---

[6]   "Ep. 215 Activate Your Prey Drive with Michael Burt." *Reminder Media Podcast.* https://remindermedia.com/podcast/ ep-215-activate-your-prey-drive-with-michael-burt.

Exposure—Who do you spend time with each day? Do those people push you to excel, or do they distract or discourage you? If you want to win, it helps to surround yourself with people who inspire or, better yet, push you to succeed.

Comparison—Comparison can work for or against you. Comparing yourself to someone else can be disheartening (and not a fair or effective way to measure your success). But understanding what's possible for you and then comparing where you are now to where you could be might just be the kind of motivation you need to stay on track.

Once you know what drives you, Coach Burt advises putting structures in place to keep your Prey Drive activated or to reactivate it regularly. "It's a muscle that you have to work every day to keep it strong," he says.

Remember, you're the narrator of your story. You can tell yourself you'll never finish, never succeed, or you can be intentional about setting up your schedule and surroundings in a way that moves you consistently and persistently toward your goal.

If your story needs a rewrite or a redirect, you're the one with the power to take your life in a different direction. You choose where to focus your attention and when to take action. As Burt says, you have the power to activate the *innate* Prey Drive and go after the life you want.

2
WHAT'S YOUR FOCUS?

What consumes your mind controls your life.

—Anonymous

Several years ago, I participated in Dan Sullivan's Strategic Coach® program. I had met a number of successful business leaders at that point in my career and had noticed that many of them were or had been participants in Strategic Coach®. As Tony Robbins says, "Success leaves clues," so when Dan Sullivan came to Atlanta (my hometown at the time), I promptly signed up for his yearlong coaching program.

One of the main themes of the comprehensive program was to determine your Unique Ability® (something we'll get into more in just a few pages). The flip side of that was to identify what took time, energy, and, thus, *focus* away from what you did best. Those were the things that could and probably should be outsourced.

That part was easy for me. Laundry was *not* my Unique Ability®. I tended to put clothes in the washer and forget about them for several days, where they soured and then needed to be rewashed. One day, I realized I could drop off my laundry, and someone else would do it for me—wash, dry, and fold—for about the price of one lunch. It was a game-changer. Knowing I could outsource that simple task (and probably should have long before) freed me to spend time on things that were more important to me—activities that I was better suited for and would make a difference in my life.

Laundry was only the beginning.

FOCUS ON YOUR SUPERPOWER

The ability to do what you've been called to do using the gifts you have is the most precious superpower you have.

—Unknown (but true, nonetheless)

If you could choose a superpower, what would it be?

A 2022 study by TransImpact found that of all the potential superpowers—from X-ray vision to flight to super-strength—the abilities to teleport and heal (others or oneself) are the most desired in the United States.[7]

Have you ever thought about what the world would be like if we *did* have Avengers-style superpowers? Almost 75 percent of the people from that same survey said they believed the world would be a better place if everyone had a superpower. And I suppose if we all used our powers for good, that would be true. But the study also found that 2.3 out of 10 males would give up their firstborn to have superpowers, so there's that.

---

[7]   Amy Nowell. "The Most Desired Superpowers Around the U.S." *TransImpact.com.* April 13, 2022. https://transimpact.com/nextsights/superpower-survey.

Teleportation may not be possible anytime soon, but you *do* have a superpower. You may be using it without even knowing it. The kicker is that you could do even more with your superpower if you recognized it for what it is.

No, it isn't the ability to leap tall buildings in a single bound. It's something far more useful than that.

So what is it?

Don't look at me for the answer. This one's all you.

Your superpower is the thing that you're best at. In the business world, it's known as your greatest strength.

Can you name it?

A lot of people can't. They haven't identified their strengths because those traits or abilities feel normal to them—like something anyone should be able to do. Those skills come so naturally to them that they don't think much about them.

Dan Sullivan, the founder of Strategic Coach‌, calls this superpower your Unique Ability‌: "Your Unique Ability is you at your best. It's the *hard-wired set of natural talents* that you're passionate about making use of in every area of your life. It honors what's already *within you*, what people count on you for, and how you create your best results."[8] [emphasis mine]

"YOUR UNIQUE ABILITY IS YOU AT YOUR BEST. IT'S THE *HARD-WIRED SET OF NATURAL TALENTS* THAT YOU'RE PASSIONATE ABOUT MAKING USE OF IN EVERY AREA OF YOUR LIFE. IT HONORS WHAT'S ALREADY *WITHIN YOU*, WHAT PEOPLE COUNT ON YOU FOR, AND HOW YOU CREATE YOUR BEST RESULTS."

—DAN SULLIVAN, FOUNDER, STRATEGIC COACH

---

[8] "A Beginners Guide to Unique Ability." Dan Sullivan, *StrategicCoach.com.* https://resources.strategiccoach.com/guides/a-beginners-guide-to-unique-ability.

Identifying your superpower is essential to your success. Unfortunately, most of us spend more time trying to improve in the areas where we are weak than we do harnessing our strengths. However, as with your mindset and the story you tell yourself, you have a choice. When you choose to recognize your strengths and how they play into where you are now and what you've already accomplished, you can build on your successes.

So what is it that you do well? What comes naturally to you? What is it that has allowed you to experience the success you have had so far?

For me, it's the ability to take risks, try new things, and figure out the *how* as I go. My resume offers evidence of the fact that I don't mind shaking things up.

My first job out of college was as a real estate agent. Then, I started a staffing company. I later joined forces with a friend and built a financial services company. Then, I founded Dry Farm Wines, and in 2022, I co-founded Zero Hunger Water. Through it all, I've experienced varying degrees of success. I've made some money and lost some money, but I've always been my own boss.

My aunt, on the other hand, worked for the state government for thirty years. One job. One employer. She looks at my life in amazement and makes comments like, "I can't believe all the things you've done!"

To me, building new businesses is just what I do. I'm an entrepreneur. I like to figure things out as I go. Uncertainty doesn't scare me. There have been times when I knew my rent was coming due and I didn't have money in the bank, but I also knew I could figure out how to get the money before the landlord came knocking. The idea of working for someone else seems like a greater risk to me because employees never know when the company execs might decide to cut jobs. Neither approach is right or wrong, but one works for me, and the other works for people like my aunt.

Your superpower is all about you and what you excel at right now, not something you have to work to improve.

Tennis pro Roger Federer's backhand, for example, was his superpower. He and his opponents knew it. His forehand, not so much. He could have spent hours practicing to improve his forehand but made a point, instead, to stick to his strengths. "In tennis, working on your weaknesses makes you maybe an overall complete player, but you won't be dangerous anymore," he said. "That's why I like to work on my strengths, and it's really helped me in my career."[9] His superpower did, in fact, make him dangerous to his opponents. He retired in 2022 with more than one hundred titles, multiple record-breaking wins, the No. 1 position of the Association of Tennis Professionals for 310 weeks (237 of those weeks consecutively), and $130,594,339 in prize money.[10]

What is it that makes you unique or even dangerous? It's those strengths and unique talents that make you as spectacular as Michelangelo's *David*. Focus on your superpower, on being and sharing your best with the world. Do that, and you'll *know* you're living out your calling.

- **How much time do you spend trying to improve in your areas of weakness?** We all have things we hate to do or legitimately stink at. Don't fall into the trap of trying to *fix* yourself in areas that don't matter. Maybe, for example, bookkeeping is not your

---

[9]   Quote from Roger Federer. "5 Life Lessons from Roger Federer In His Own Words." *Tennis Express*. Tennis Now. September 27, 2016. YouTube. https://youtu.be/lZAvaVZ69Bg.

[10] Roger Federer. Wikipedia. https://en.wikipedia.org/wiki/Roger_Federer.

thing. Instead of spending hours doing that task, consider delegating it so you can focus your time and energy on the things that bring you the greatest joy, success, and profit.

- **What are you the best at?** Give yourself some credit! If you honestly don't know what your strengths or Unique Abilities are, use a tool like the Kolbe Assessment or CliftonStrengths' Assessment to determine your areas of greatness. You might even ask your friends or colleagues what they see as your greatest assets.

- **What are the talents or personality traits that have helped you create success in your life?** We build on our successes. Recognizing what has allowed you to excel in the past can help you determine what you might want to do more of—the skills or habits that you want to harness and hone.

WHY FOCUS CAN BE DIFFICULT

Your most important resource is your attention. What you pay attention to determines what happens differently in your life.

—Robert Cooper

Focus is powerful and rare. Stats vary on the average person's attention span—from a mere eight seconds to a few hours. What about you? How long can you focus on, well, anything with your complete attention without multi-tasking, picking up your phone to check messages or social media updates, or following drifting thoughts about what's for dinner tonight?

Chances are, you didn't make it through these few opening lines without your mind wandering from the page.

Don't worry, I won't take that personally.

The truth is your brain seeks out distractions. Millennia ago, the innate hyper-awareness of changes to one's environment served an important purpose: survival. You never knew when danger would arise in the form of a hungry lion looking for supper. Being on high alert kept you alive. Granted, there are probably some places in the world where that skill may still come in hand, but for those of us living in safe, comfortable homes and working in tidy offices, there's no longer a need for that kind of vigilance, and yet the brain remains on high alert. Today, however, it's mainly looking for distractions.

Technology is a common form of distraction and gets a lot of flak for the loss of the average person's attention span. Smartphones are only one of countless ways to satisfy the brain's craving for stimuli. Regardless of whether distractions are external (interruptions caused by coworkers, kids, or pets) or internal (our own wandering minds), the effect is the same. "We live in a world in which partial, limited attention is about all we can muster most of the time," says neuroscientist Robert Cooper.[11] And our brains like it that way.

At the same time that the brain is seeking distractions, it's also working to maintain the status quo. The human brain actively resists change. "Your brain automates everything it can; it almost always reacts negatively to anything different, and it can only focus in short bursts of attention," Cooper explained during a leadership training event.[12]

---

[11] *"UPWIRE #56 - Attention, Distractions and the Human Brain." Upwire: Hacking Human Nature* Podcast. 20/21/2015. https://archive.org/details/podcast_upwire-hacking-human-nature_upwire-56-attention-distra_1000355076138.

[12] Cooper, Robert. "Robert Cooper, PhD - Leadership Training," https://vimeo.com/162532603.

The brain's tendency to seek stimulation combined with its propensity to avoid change so it can run your life on autopilot is a double hit on your ability to focus and even more so on your stamina for self-improvement. You may want to change something about yourself or plan to reach a big goal, but your brain wants to keep things running the way they have been. The reason? Habitual behaviors are easy to maintain. The brain has a pattern to follow, and sticking to it requires very little energy. Beyond that, concentrated attention is essential to advancing important goals or changing ingrained behaviors or mindsets. That kind of focus is challenging when the brain is on the lookout for distractions.

See the dilemma?

The good news is that change is possible. "You and I have within us . . . this vast, untapped peak capacity, and all you and I have to do is unlock it, and it will take on a life all its own. It will grow us and engage us with the world, with learning, with life differently," Cooper said.

But how do we tap into that capacity?

As with most things, it comes down to a choice.

YOU GET TO CHOOSE YOUR FOCUS

"You're just wearing rose-colored glasses. You only see the good." Exasperation laced with disgust dripped from my friend's words.

Actually, "friend" is a bit of an overstatement. We were friendly, but lately, I'd been doing all I could to avoid him. Our conversation that day reminded me of why.

You know the people whose presence just makes you feel good? The ones who light up the room when they walk in?

Well, this guy was the opposite. You felt the mood lighten when he left the room.

I'm not being cruel or judgmental; I have simply learned that there are people I don't want to hang out with. People who bring negativity into my life, for example. Or people, like this guy, who have a knack for finding the worst in any situation, the flaw in any plan, and the downside of any idea.

I don't remember the topic of our conversation that day, but I do remember my response: "Well, I am looking for it!"

Listen, I'd rather wear rose-colored glasses than live in the dark. I'd rather look for the best and find it than look for the worst and find that.

I'D RATHER WEAR ROSE-COLORED GLASSES THAN LIVE IN THE DARK. I'D RATHER LOOK FOR THE BEST AND FIND IT THAN LOOK FOR THE WORST AND FIND THAT.

You'll find whatever you look for. That is true no matter who you are or where you're from.

Want to find happiness? Keep your eyes open for it.

Want to find the flaws? They're there, and you don't have to look very far or hard before you see something wrong with the world.

I am a big fan of believing that for as complicated as this world is, there's more than enough good to go around. And most of the time, the easiest way to find good is simply to look for it. Point it out. Share a little joy with the people around you. They need it. Everyone does—including you!

Maybe you're like my friend and, right about now, are feeling annoyed at the simplicity of this philosophy. There's so much bad in the world! How can you expect me to just ignore it?

First off, yes, there are all sorts of bad in this world: Bad people who make bad decisions and create bad situations for the rest of us. If you scroll through any social media platform or turn on any news station, you'll find example after terrible example of what's wrong with the world. Consume enough of that negative content, and you'll start to believe the sky is falling and that bad guys, cancer, and financial ruin are just around the corner.

There's a reason some therapists and countless life coaches recommend that their clients limit or eliminate the news from their daily media diet. Constant negative messaging affects your mental well-being, and those effects can stay with you for hours. A steady diet of bad news can end up changing your outlook on life.

Some people balk at the idea of cutting out news media. You might be one of them and think that turning off the news is equivalent to sticking your head in the sand and pretending everything is fine. And I get it. I watch the news because I want to be informed. That's true for a lot of people. As one psychologist puts it, staying informed is an attempt at self-preservation. "News appeals to your mind's quest for survival-relevant information, but it doesn't necessarily meet that need. It squanders your attention on generalized threats signals that you can't really act on," says Loretta Graziano Breuning, author of *Habits of a Happy Brain*. Rather than filling your mind with distressing details over which you have little to no control, she says, "You are better off gathering your own information to navigate your own obstacles."[13]

Attune your focus to what's relevant to your life—the life you want to live—and seek out information sources that equip you to move toward your goals. The news, which is broad,

---

[13]   Loretta Graziano Breuning. "Stop Traumatizing Yourself by Watching the News." *PsychologyToday.com*. October 29, 2014. https://www.psychologytoday.com/us/blog/your-neurochemical-self/201410/stop-traumatizing-yourself-watching-the-news.

random, and largely negative, is probably not the best source for motivation. Limiting your exposure to negative influences, be it the Debbie Downers in your life or the virtual spaces where people love to complain, can clear the way for you to see what's right with the world and greater possibilities for your future.

- What are you looking for? You can find the negative in anything. If all you're looking for is what won't work or reasons why something or someone will fail, that's what you'll find. The contrast is also true.

- What do you want to find? If you're tired of seeing all the negativity in this world, stop looking for it as if you're on a treasure hunt. What do you want to find or experience more of in your life?

- Whom or what are you allowing to control your attention? There's a popular (and true) statement claiming that "What consumes your mind controls your life." What or who gets most of your attention? Is that what you want to control your life?

HOW: TRAIN YOUR BRAIN TO FOCUS ON WHAT YOU WANT

Whatever good things we build end up building us.

—Jim Rohn

A few years back, a little book titled *The Secret* cast the personal development industry under its spell. To date, more than thirty million copies of the book are circulating the globe in fifty different languages.[14] The film by the same name brought in $65.6 million at the box office.[15] With the secret out, it seems like everyone in the world ought to have exactly what they want, right?

You and I both know that's not the case. And you know how I feel about the "secret" to success. For all the hype around the book and film, however, it turns out that there is some actual science behind the message. The "universe" may or may not be looking out for you, but you can bet your brain will *if* you ask it to.

The Secret is based on the philosophy of The Law of Attraction, where like attracts like. Sometimes, the over-simplification of "think good thoughts and good things will happen" is admittedly a little hard to swallow. But when you add neuroscience into the equation, The Law of Attraction seems less "woo-woo" and instead downright viable because of something called your "Reticular Activating System" or RAS.

RAS = YOUR BRAIN'S FOCUS FILTER

Your amazing brain can process an unfathomable 11 million bits of information every second: every sound your house makes, the lights around you, what time of day it is, the train in the distance, the temperature of the air, your body's basic functions—from your heartbeat and blood flow to working on healing the blister you got on a hike or knowing when to breathe so that your brain and body gets the oxygen it

---

[14]   The Secret (Byrne book). https://en.m.wikipedia.org/wiki/The_Secret_(Byrne_book)#:~:text=The%20book%20has%20sold%2030,been%20translated%20into%2050%20languages

[15]   https://en.m.wikipedia.org/wiki/The_Secret_(2006_film)

needs—and so much more. The conscious brain, however, can only manage to process 40 to 50 bits of information per second.[16]

Because paying attention to 11 million bits of information per second is impossible, your reticular activating system filters out all but what your conscious mind can handle. Here's the essential idea you need to understand: Your brain chooses what to filter out based on what it deems important—and *you can tell your brain what's important.* That's the "secret" in a nutshell. That's how you tap into that vast capacity Cooper talks about.

> YOUR BRAIN CHOOSES WHAT TO FILTER OUT BASED ON WHAT IT DEEMS IMPORTANT— AND *YOU CAN TELL YOUR BRAIN WHAT'S IMPORTANT.*

A simple example of this that I'm sure you've experienced is the phenomenon that occurs when you buy a new car. If you buy a blue Buick, suddenly you start seeing blue Buicks everywhere. They were always there, but now they mean something to you, and your brain pays attention and makes sure you notice them.

This whole chapter has been about being intentional with the way you think about the world and yourself because your thoughts matter. They are powerful. And you *can* change them if they aren't serving you well. You can also use your thoughts to program your RAS to allow your conscious mind to become aware of information and opportunities that are relevant to you. In fact, you're already doing that whether you realize it or not. Your RAS is the reason you find what you're looking

---

[16] "Understanding Unconscious Bias." *Short Wave.* July 15, 2020. https://www.npr.org/2020/07/14/891140598/ understanding-unconscious-bias.

for in life (good or bad). Your thoughts are telling your brain to watch for and make you aware of.

The problem for a lot of people, however, is that they allow their brains to run on default—automating everything it can and maintaining the status quo—because that's what's easy. As Cooper explains, even though it seems like doing the same thing day after day should get the same result, the reality is that nothing stays the same, including your brain.

Your brain changes every day. It makes thousands of new brain cells as it processes unending amounts of data. Growing up, I was taught that you have the maximum number of brain cells you will ever have by the time you're eighteen. That message followed me into adulthood and, with it, a sense of despair. If brain growth stopped at eighteen *and* we lost some of those precious cells every day, it was all downhill from eighteen on. Even when I was eighteen, I didn't want that adolescent year to be my peak of brain potential.

Current science shows that the brain is constantly renewing itself. More than that, it has the ability to change through neuroplasticity. That means you can change your beliefs by thinking new thoughts and creating new habits. If you make the choice to think differently and have more productive thoughts, your body will reward you. Your brain will participate in that choice by *helping* you think more positive and productive thoughts.

If you help the brain, it will help you. If you're intentional with your learning, being, and thinking, you improve.

The opposite is also true. If you're negligent or hands-off, your brain, your body, and your life get lazy, unhealthy, and stagnant. Without your focused direction, the brain declines because it wants to do what's easy. The result, Cooper notes, is that "You do more of what you do. You think more the way you think. You react the more the way you always react. And you settle into 'that's just the way I am,' as the world changes and leaves you behind."[17]

PROGRAM YOUR RAS TO CHOOSE WISELY

Growing is a choice. You can have all the information and tools and every advantage at your disposal, but if you choose not to use them—or just fail to acknowledge them—nothing changes. Remember: Knowledge isn't power. Acting on that knowledge is what makes a difference. You and your choices are the deciding factors in the way your life progresses. Programming your RAS helps make the right options obvious and easier to choose. Here are three ways you can do that.

1. **Make your brain aware of what you want through visualization.** Visualize the outcome you desire. Record-setting, medal-winning athletes regularly practice visualization. They create a mental picture of the ball going through the hoop, or making a hole in one, or sticking the landing perfectly. The same approach can work for you and your goals. Visualize yourself enjoying the kind of relationships you want, responding thoughtfully to conflict, feeling healthy and fit, making the sale, or doing whatever it is that is important to you.

   When you visualize what you want, you're telling RAS what to filter in. What you want gets embedded into your subconscious, and your brain starts working *for* you instead of sticking to default patterns that work against you. Rather than spending all its effort seeking distractions, your brain will look for ways to make your goals a reality, alerting you to

---

[17] Robert Cooper Ph.D. - Leadership Training, https://vimeo.com/162532603.

opportunities you may have missed before and filtering out what doesn't help you win. It will also make the right choices a little easier. Right when you're about to grab that second serving of dessert, your brain will recall that fit and healthy image you've created to remind you of your goal.

As with most self-improvement and goal-reaching strategies, repetition is important. Visualization is not a one-and-done technique. To effectively keep your RAS alert to things you want to bring into your life, you'll need to visualize those things daily—even if it's just for five to ten minutes a day.

Some people do this by rewriting their goals every day. Some create vision boards. Do what works for you to bring into focus what matters most.

2. **Start your day with purpose.** "The first twenty-one minutes of the day sets in motion your entire day," Cooper says. Visualization can be part of that, as can other positive mental and physical practices. Here are some habits to consider adding to your morning routine:

    - Start the day with a focused mind by meditating for a few minutes.

    - Drink a cup of water. Your brain is approximately 75 percent water. Even a small amount of dehydration can impair its function, which makes it easy to slip back into old patterns.[18]

    - Practice gratitude.

    - Review your goals. Practice visualizing your success.

---

[18] Majid Fotuhi. "Hydration is Key: Water your brain." Neurogrow.com. December 10, 2019. https://neurogrow.com/water-your-brain/.

- Determine your top priorities for the day.

- Do something for your physical health—exercise, stretch, yoga, breathe.

3. **Opt for change or challenge.** Your brain wants to maintain the status quo, but when you opt to lean into change or challenge with curiosity and openness, you grow. Your brain will eventually understand that change isn't necessarily a threat that needs to be avoided. The more you do hard things, the easier it becomes to take on and overcome challenges.

Change is a choice, and you are the only one who can make the right choice for you. So choose wisely.

3

WHO IS YOUR WORST ENEMY?

You yourself will always be the worst enemy you can encounter; you yourself lie in wait for yourself in caves and forests.

—*Friedrich Nietzsche*

You've probably heard the phrase *be yourself, everyone else taken*. A story I read years ago really coalesced that advice for me. In an interview for *People*, Oprah Winfrey said, "When I auditioned for my first television job, I walked in not knowing what to do, so I pretended to be Barbara Walters, I pretended to be her. I sat like Barbara. I crossed my legs like Barbara. I tried to talk like Barbara. I had Barbara in my head for about a year until one night I mispronounced Canada and called it Ca-nada. And that is not what Barbara Walters would do. And it was the first time I had a breakthrough to be myself."[19]

---

[19] Sullivan, Marisa. "Oprah Winfrey Credits Barbara Walters for the Start of Her Career: 'I Pretended to Be Her.'" *People*. December 31,

Like Oprah early in her career, sometimes you may believe you have to be like someone else to be accepted or get noticed. When really, all you have to do is *just be yourself.*

It sounds like such simple advice, doesn't it? After all, who else are you going to be?

Well, people have a lot of ideas about your options these days. Maybe you've seen the memes:

Just be yourself. Unless you can be a unicorn. Then always be a unicorn. (Variations: dragon, dinosaur, hamster, goose, turtles . . . . The desire to be an animal—imaginary, extinct, or real—is strong with some folks. My dog has a pretty good life, so maybe that's not such a bad idea.)

Just be yourself. Unless you can be a captain. Then you should always be a captain. (Variations: Batman, a Jedi, or the best yet, Jedi Betty White. There's something to be said, I suppose, for possessing unquestionable power or authority.)

But my favorite of these memes has been repeated with slight variations by quite a few people, including author and humorist David Sedaris during a commencement speech at Oberlin College and Conservatory: "Just be yourself unless yourself is an asshole."[20] Sedaris went on to give the graduates a few hints for how to know if they were a decent person—something most people want to be and generally assume they are. (Although sometimes we know they're wrong.)

Mike Rowe, known best as the host of *Dirty Jobs,* where he highlights vocations that are a bit less sanitized than my own career choices, commented in a Facebook post about the reality that being yourself might not always be a good thing.

2022. https://people.com/tv/oprah-winfrey-credits-barbara-walters-for-the-start-of-her-career-i-pretended-to-be-her/

[20] Sedaris, David. "A Few Words to the Graduates." *The Paris Review.* June 11, 2018. https://www.theparisreview.org/blog/2018/06/11/a-few-words-to-the-graduates/.

Sometimes, in fact, a lot of the time, we (and the world around us) might be better off if *we* were *better*:

Mystic Meaning writes:

Dear Mike,

I'm amazed by what you've created here. It's an inspiration to see how a guy who is really just being himself can generate this tsunami of love and admiration. But being yourself, as odd as it sounds, takes practice. It takes knowing who you are, as Socrates says. This seems to be what you have done. Do you have any thoughts on what it takes to be yourself, the practice of it, the work of it? As paradoxical as it sounds, do you think people need to spend more time "working out" their "true self muscles?"

Hi Mystic,

Thanks for the kind words. It's been fun to watch this place grow, and while I'm flattered by your suggestion that "being myself" is the sole reason, I'm afraid you may have overestimated my natural charms. Like most people on Planet Earth, I was born lazy, helpless, greedy, and selfish, and I'm pretty sure I'd still be that way if my parents hadn't insisted I become something less obnoxious. The degree to which they succeeded is debatable, but with respect to the whole nature/nurture conversation, one thing has become obvious to me over the years—being myself is easy. Being someone better is not.

Rowe went on to say that terrible people, including Hitler, Stalin, Jim Jones, Osama Bin Laden, "and millions of lesser-known creeps and villains currently serving time in prison" were all just being themselves. Even people who aren't evil—people like you and I—may occasionally do or say things that come across to others as hurtful, frustrating, or irritating when we're just being ourselves. Habitually doing those things can damage relationships, cost you a job, or worse. So what's the solution? Rowe's advice is simple:

> My philosophy is this: If you want to be less of an ass-hole, stop acting like one. If you want more people to like you, do more likable things. Regardless of all the personal enlightenment, we're not judged in this life by what we discover within ourselves or what we come to believe—we're only judged on what we do.[21]

The challenge is that it is impossible to make everyone happy. In an effort to be authentic, we're going to irritate or even anger a few people. Trying to pacify everyone is both exhausting and completely inauthentic. That's not a license to forego kindness and compassion for others. Those traits ought to be traits we strive for regardless of anything else. Nor does the commitment to authenticity mean that we should waive responsibilities. We have obligations as citizens of the human race.

To authentically be who we are—or who we *want* to be— we have to act in ways that align with our *best* selves while giving those around us the freedom to do the same (even if those people irritate us). Which is why authenticity isn't easy to master.

But here's what I know about you: You are reading a book about how to be better. That right there says something great about you: You want to be the *best,* most authentic version of

---

[21]   Rowe, Mike. "Of Authenticity and Assholes." Facebook.com/. March 22, 2015. https://www.facebook.com/TheRealMikeRowe/ photos/of-assholes-and-authenticitymystic-meaning-writesdea r-mikeim-amazed-by-what-youv/963186413691502/.

yourself. That takes commitment and work because, as Rowe noted, being yourself is easy. "Being someone better is not."

BE YOURSELF. (ONLY BETTER.)

If you want things to change, YOU have to change.
If you will change, everything will change for you.

—Jim Rohn

Being better doesn't mean you have to be a unicorn or Batman or Jedi Betty White. Nor should you try to be *anyone* other than yourself, which is where so many of us get tripped up. With all the time the world spends watching what other people do, how they look, what they wear, and what they eat, it can be easy to fall into the trap of believing that being *better* means being like someone else.

Appearances, however, are deceiving, especially when it comes to what we see on social media (or TV or movies, etc.). I have friends who occasionally take breaks from social media because scrolling through proof that everyone else's life is perfect leaves them feeling depressed.

What we all need to remember is that other person's post is *one millisecond* out of his or her day. Someone shares a pic of a delicious-looking slice of pie that makes you salivate, and then you start wondering how they can eat that way and still look like they do—and why you can't. Someone else posts about having a solid day when your day started with a flat tire.

Comparison robs you of joy and assures you that your life will never measure up. It tricks you into believing that you will never be good enough. We know that's not true.

But what if everyone took their pictures in iPhone's Live mode and posted the three seconds before or after that perfect moment? I'll tell you what would happen because I've seen it. That one picture-perfect millisecond is surrounded by frustrated arguments, self-deprecating words, and silent insecurities (*I hate my hair. Gotta suck in that gut. I hope my ex sees this!*).

The carefully curated images we see in the media are only part of the story. If you saw the whole story—the truth about what goes on when the camera's off—you might feel a little better about yourself and a lot more satisfied with your life.

No, being better isn't about being like anyone else. It starts with recognizing and then amplifying the best parts of who you are. Remember those superpowers you identified in the previous chapter? It's time to use them!

> BEING BETTER ISN'T ABOUT BEING LIKE ANYONE ELSE. IT STARTS WITH RECOGNIZING AND THEN AMPLIFYING THE BEST PARTS OF WHO YOU ARE.

Being better also means you take the time to acknowledge the areas in your life where you want (or even *need*) to make some changes—and then *actually make those changes*. It's one thing to be aware of. It's something altogether different to take action, and action is what this book is all about. Socrates believed so much in the value of personal reflection that he claimed the unexamined life was not worth living. Reflection *is* an essential practice for a well-lived life, but if you don't do something about what you learn, things will never improve.

- **What is keeping you from being yourself?** *Just be yourself* can sound like irritatingly trite advice if you're afraid that who you are isn't good enough. Everyone wants to feel loved, and to be loved is to be known. When you're constantly worried that people wouldn't like the real you, that they would shun or think less of you because of your quirks, your unique personality, your affinity for some obscure hobby, or your habit of leaving your socks on the floor, you'll hide who you are from the rest of the world. What is it that you're afraid people might discover if they knew the real you?

- **Would you look down on someone else if they had the same quirk, personality trait, hobby, or habit?** Humans are great at projecting. We *think* we know what other people will say or how they will respond to us, so we put up walls to deflect potential rejection and protect ourselves emotionally from disappointment. Self-induced shame and embarrassment keep us from letting others see beyond those walls. In other words, we're afraid to be ourselves around others because we assume they'll reject us. The question to ask yourself is this: Would you reject someone for the same reason? If not, it's time to let people in. Start with the people who love you.

- **What do you need to change?** If you *would* reject someone who had the same traits or flaws as you, then it might be time to consider changing that habit. If you don't like the fact that you're a slob, stop being a slob. (Put your dirty socks in the hamper!) Or maybe it's more serious than a messy house. You may have a habit of lying, for example. You wouldn't want others to lie to you. You might even disassociate yourself from people you feel you can't trust. Well, guess what? Lying is an asshole trait. Stop it.

YOU HAVE THE POWER TO BECOME YOUR BEST SELF

Man stands in his own shadow and wonders why it's dark.

—Zen saying

The truth about change is that it can seem difficult, but it doesn't have to be.

Here's why change can seem hard: Mental and physical patterns of behaviors and thoughts—our habits—make it possible for us to run on autopilot. Based on current brain research, humans have an average of 6,200 thoughts a day or about six-and-a-half thoughts a minute.[22]

When those thoughts run unchecked, they race toward negativity. But it's not your fault if your thoughts trend negative. Your brain likes it that way.

Negative thoughts, such as those focused on self-doubt, worries, fears, and external threats, invite the nervous system to dose the brain with cortisol—a stress hormone that is part of your survival response. (Think fight, flight, or freeze.) The brain loves cortisol. Left to itself, the brain accepts every opportunity for a hit, and the steady dosing can be detrimental to your health. When the body is constantly flooded with cortisol, the effect is an increased risk for a host of health issues, including the following:

---

[22] Raypole, Crystal. "How Many Thoughts Do You Have Each Day? And Other Things to Think About." Healthline.com. February 28, 2022. https://www.healthline.com/health/how-many-thoughts-per-day#thoughts-per-day.

- Anxiety

- Depression

- Digestive problems

- Headaches

- Muscle tension and pain

- Heart disease, heart attack, high blood pressure, and stroke

- Sleep problems

- Weight gain

- Memory and concentration impairment[23]

Positive or uplifting thoughts, on the other hand, can trigger the release of serotonin and dopamine. Dopamine controls your motivation, and serotonin is what makes you feel happy. But certain health issues (some of them fairly common) can create dopamine and serotonin deficiencies. Additionally, cortisol itself can deplete both serotonin and dopamine levels, creating a double hit on how you feel, think, and act. Studies show that women with low serotonin levels are prone to depression, anxiety, and binge eating. Men who are low in serotonin are more inclined toward alcoholism, ADHD, and impulse control issues. When your dopamine

[23] "Chronic stress puts your health at risk." *Mayo Clinic.* July 08, 2021. https://www.mayoclinic.org/healthy-lifestyle/stress-management/in-depth/stress/art-20046037#:~:text=Cortisol%2C%20the%20primary%20stress%20hormone,fight%2Dor%2Dflight%20situation.

levels are low, you end up feeling lethargic, unmotivated, and generally uninspired.[24]

Because our brains like consistency and predictability, we tend to think the same things over and over again. If those repeated thoughts are negative, the cycle continues: Cortisol increases while levels of dopamine and serotonin decrease.

The effect is that you become your own worst enemy.

You *think* you can't, so you don't even try.

You *think* you aren't worthy of good things, so you don't expect good things to happen.

You *think* you've been handed a raw deal and act accordingly.

You *think* you aren't important and aren't making a difference, and you wonder, *what's the point?*

Here's the good news: *You have the power to change the way you think.* You can shift your thoughts from those of doubt and discouragement to an internal conversation that is uplifting and empowering.

No one talks more to you than you do, so you've got to pay attention to what you say, especially if you want to change anything about yourself or your life. But you have to *want* to change.

HOW: NEURO-LINGUISTIC PROGRAMMING

Our ability to do anything in life is based on our ability to direct our nervous system.

—Tony Robbins

My two favorite forms of performance entertainment are stand-up comedy and live music concerts. Why? Because

---

[24] "Chronic Stress — The Effects on Your Brain." Australian Spinal Research Foundation. June 30, 2016. https://spinalresearch.com.au/chronic-stress-effects-brain.

besides being enjoyable, comedians and musicians have the incredible power to change people's physiology. You can be in the audience, one hundred feet away, and a good stand-up comic's joke will reach you from the stage and bring you to tears with laughter. That's magical!

Musicians have a similar power. If you've been to a concert and *felt* the emotion of the song, you know what I'm referring to. Maybe you were moved to dance or to sing the lyrics at the top of your lungs. Or maybe the words and melody just ripped your heart out. You can be in the middle of tens of thousands of people, hundreds of yards from the performer, and without touching you physically, the musician alters your mood and posture and can make you act like a complete fool without a care in the world. That's what I call powerful!

Our language, thoughts, and behavior are all interconnected. Outside forces can influence them, like the comedian who makes you laugh until tears roll down your cheeks or the musician who moves you to throw your hands in the air and dance with abandon. Notice that in both of these examples, no one *makes* you respond. The musician doesn't come to your seat, pull you up, and force you to dance. The power is the transfer of emotion, thought, and energy. The mental state the music or humor puts you in elicits a physical response.

But there's a more powerful and constant force that influences your language, thoughts, and behaviors and the way they affect your life.

That force is *you*.

THE MIND-BODY CONNECTION

Back in the late 1980s, Robert Dilts, a leading behavioral skills trainer and business consultant, identified six ways the brain's thoughts and emotions work together to affect the body's nervous system and create a variety of physical responses. He named the model NeuroLogical Levels, and to varying degrees, those six levels are all within your control.

THE SIX NEUROLOGICAL LEVELS AND WHAT EACH AFFECTS

1. **Spirit**—This level refers to our sense of purpose and meaning in life and our sense of being connected to something larger than ourselves. **It affects** your nervous system, life-sustaining functions, and reticular system.

2. **Identity**—This level relates to our sense of self: who we are and what we understand our roles in life to be. **It affects** your immune and endocrine system— the nervous system as a whole— as well as your reticular system.

3. **Beliefs and values**—This level relates to the thoughts and judgments that guide the way we evaluate ourselves and the world. **It affects** your limbic and autonomic control system (e.g., heart rate and other unconscious responses).

4. **Capabilities**—This level refers to "mental maps" or mental strategies that guide our responses and behaviors. Capabilities are developed over time and differ from involuntary reactions. **It affects** your cortical system (e.g., semi-conscious actions, including eye movement and posture).

5. **Behaviors**—This level refers to the way we physically interact with or respond to others and our environments. **It affects** your motor systems or conscious actions.

6. **Environment**—This level refers to the physical surroundings, including the temperature and noise level
of the room and other external conditions. **It affects**
your peripheral nervous system (your sensations and
reflex actions).[25]

So, why does this matter? Why do we need to understand this
interconnection of the body, mind, and spirit? The simplest
answer is because this deep and unbreakable connection, which
you influence with your words, thoughts, and actions, affects
every aspect of your life.

This is why what you say to and about yourself, others, and
the world matters. Your words may be intangible, but they have
power. Maya Angelou put it this way in a conversation with
comedian Dave Chappell, "I believe that a word is a thing.
It is non-visible. It is audible only for the time it's there. It
hangs in the air. But I believe it is a thing. I believe it goes
into the upholstery. And then into the rugs, and into my hair,
and into my clothes, and then finally into my body. I believe
that words are things. And I live on them."[26]

What words are you living on?

USING NLP TO MASTER YOUR THOUGHTS, FEELINGS, AND ACTIONS

Neuro-Linguistic Programming, or NLP, is the tool or method
many coaches and some therapists have used for decades to
empower people to direct their nervous system, changing their
behaviors and, consequently, the outcomes they achieve. If

25 Dilts, Robert. "A Brief History of Logical Levels." http://www.nlpu.com/Articles/LevelsSummary.htm. 2014. Accessed 12/2023.
26 Angelou, Maya. *Iconoclasts: Dave Chapelle and Maya Angelou.* Racial Media. November 30, 2006.

you've ever wondered how Tony Robbins gets people to walk on coals without being burned, overcome life-long phobias in a matter of minutes, or break addictions and bad habits, NLP is the answer.

NLP is a multifaceted tool and can be used in a number of different ways, but the bottom line is that you change the way you feel about and respond to something by changing the way you think and speak about that thing. You either change *what* you think (flipping a worst-case scenario around and imagining the best-case scenario instead), or you can change *how* you think about something (replacing negative feelings about something with positive imagery, thoughts, and emotions). Both approaches use visualization and reframing techniques that may engage any or all of the physical senses. Tony Robbins explains, "Our ability to do anything in life is based on our ability to direct our nervous system. Those who are able to produce some outstanding results do so by producing specific communication to and through the nervous system."[27]

In the case of a bad habit, for instance, an NLP practitioner might have the client connect the behavior with negative feelings, thoughts, and sensations through a series of visualization exercises. Eventually, the negative emotions about the habit can become so strong that the thought of engaging in the activity physically and emotionally repulses the client.

Another way you can use NLP is to silence or nullify negative self-talk. If the voice in your head responds to a big goal you've set (or want to set) with a discouraging, *You can't do that!* Robbins suggests changing the voice. Turn down the volume. "Make the voice in your head softer, farther away, and weaker." Or change the tone of the voice. "Hear it say the same things, only in a sexy voice, in an almost flirtatious

---

[27] Robbins, Anthony. *Unlimited Power.* New York: Ballantine Books, 1986.

tone and tempo: 'You can't do that.' How does it feel now? You may feel that you're even more motivated to do what the voice is telling you not to do," Robbins says. Alternatively, you change the tone to something ridiculous, like a cartoon character's voice. Any of those options negate the power of that nagging voice and make it easy to discount so you can get on with life.

You don't have to be your own worst enemy. In fact, by controlling your mind—its thoughts, feelings, and responses—you can be your greatest advocate and your best self.

4

YOU DECIDE

Teenage me: Don't tell me what to do.

Adult me: Will someone PLEASE tell me what to do?

Don't tell me what to do. It's the theme of teenagers everywhere.

To be fair, those awkward, bad-skinned, and braces years are when people are trying to figure out who they are. Teens crave freedom, and the world—from parents to teachers and even friends—can feel oppressive.

Parent: Make your bed.

Teen: *Why, I'll just mess it up again tonight!*

Mom: Why are you eating out of the saucepan? Put that macaroni and cheese in a bowl!

Teen: *Why? That will just dirty up another dish that I will have to wash later.* (True story.)

Dad: What are you wearing?

49

Teen: *What? I like it!*

Teacher: Your 1,000-word essay on *Fahrenheit 451* is due tomorrow.
Teen: *Seriously? I haven't even read the book!*

Parents: Be home by 10.
Teen: (Eye roll.)

Don't tell me what to do!

Somewhere between high school graduation and the rest of life, things change. The reality dawns that we don't have all the answers. We start looking around for someone—*anyone*—who will give us a clue to the answers to all kinds of questions:

What should I do with my life?
Why can't I figure out what I want?
How should I invest my money?
How do I tell someone how I feel?
How am I going to get over that relationship?
I know I screwed up, but how do I make things right?
What should I have for dinner?

From the existential to the mundane, we need answers!
Finding the answers to some of those questions is easy enough. You can hire a financial advisor to get your investment accounts in order. A quick search for "what's for dinner" on Google offers countless recipes and a list of local restaurants ranked by distance and customer reviews. Easy enough.
There are some questions, though, that only you can answer. Sure, a good life coach or counselor can help you work through the hard questions. But in the end, the answers come from you. You have to decide . . .

- what kind of education to pursue.

- whether you want to continue seeing that person.

- that you are worth being treated well by family members, friends, colleagues, and most importantly yourself.

- whether changing careers or starting something new is worth the risk.

- if you're going to let something (a failure or success, a criticism, a habit) define you or determine the course of your life.

- what kind of person you want to be.

You have to decide. And once you decide, you have to be the one to change your behavior to get the results you want.

Bottom line: You are in control of your destiny. To paraphrase the line from *Invictus*, you are the master of your fate. You are the captain of your soul.[28]

RESPONSIBILITY. NOT BLAME.

If anyone is magically going to appear and just suddenly make your life better, just know that person is always going to be you.

—Brianna Pastor, **author of** *Good Grief*

Now, you may be wondering, *If I am in control of my destiny, why is my life the way it is? I don't want to be unhappy, stressed*

---

[28] Henley, William Earnest. "Invictus." *Book of Verses*. 1888.

out, overweight, overworked and underpaid, in a rotten rela-
tionship, or ____(you fill in the blank)____?

The answer: Your previous choices have created the life you currently have.

That may sound harsh, but I don't mean for it to be. And before we go any further, I need to be clear: I'm not saying that if you have cancer, it's because you chose it. We live in a world where bad things happen to good people, and you may be one of those people.

You may have grown up with terrible parents who abused you physically, emotionally, or both. That's not your fault. You were a child who didn't deserve to be treated with anything less than unconditional love.

You may have been in an accident, and because of someone else's carelessness or negligence, you carry physical scars or deal with chronic pain. That's not your fault. You can't control the world or the people around you. When the wrong people cross your path, they can leave a wake of destruction behind them.

Even if the things that have happened in your past are not your *fault,* the way you choose to respond to those things is always up to you. Viktor Frankl wrote about this choice in his book *Man's Search for Meaning* after enduring imprisonment in Nazi concentration camps in World War II. Stephen Covey later noted that Frankl's choice to decide how the horror of being in those camps affected him—which was the only choice he had—allowed him to leave with his identity intact. "Between stimulus and response is our greatest power—the freedom to choose," Covey wrote.[29]

You have the same power and freedom to choose how life's circumstances will affect you. Sometimes, that ability

---

[29] Covey, Stephen R. *The Seven Habits of Highly Effective People.* Simon & Schuster: New York. 1989.

to choose your response may seem like the only power you have over those circumstances.

But you do have a choice.

You can choose to dwell on the past, feel sorry for yourself, or soak yourself in regret. *Or* you can choose to respond to unfortunate (even horrific) situations and circumstances in ways that move your life forward.

It's your choice.

More than that, it's your responsibility to respond with courage, kindness, and compassion toward yourself—to pick yourself up, get the help you need, and put those regrets behind you. No one else is going to fix your life for you.

This is *your* life. If you hand over your happiness to someone or something that hurt you, they win. Don't *ever* let that happen.

Choose to take responsibility for the way you respond to whatever life throws at you.

Choose freedom.

Choose to move forward.

If you're going to take responsibility and move forward, you'll also have to let go of blame.

Blame is part of the American psyche. *Someone must pay! Justice must be served!*

I'm not saying there shouldn't be repercussions for the people who do bad things. Rapists, murderers, drunk drivers, con artists, and other users and abusers should face consequences. No question. Sometimes, those are legal consequences. Other times, the consequence is a broken relationship. (You don't have to do life or business with people who continually hurt, cheat, or try to manipulate you.) File the complaint, hire the lawyer, give your two-weeks notice, or block their numbers.

And then move on. I know it isn't always easy, but it is for the best.

The need to lay blame can keep you stuck, reliving the moment, the conversation, the hurt over and over again. That's not productive. You can't move forward with life if you're holding on to past hurts until justice is served or the other person apologizes—because that may never happen.

Letting go of blame, much like taking responsibility for your response, puts you in a position of power. It stops other people or your circumstances from stealing your energy, your joy—your *life*.

> LETTING GO OF BLAME, MUCH LIKE TAKING RESPONSIBILITY FOR YOUR RESPONSE, PUTS YOU IN A POSITION OF POWER. IT STOPS OTHER PEOPLE OR YOUR CIRCUMSTANCES FROM STEALING YOUR ENERGY, YOUR JOY—YOUR *LIFE*.

I hadn't thought much about the consequences of blame until I heard Tony Robbins speak at Date with Destiny in 2016. He commented that the No. 1 addiction in America isn't drugs or alcohol. It's problems. "People are addicted to their problems!" he said. And he's right.

How often have you heard (or said) any of the following blame statements:

I blame the economy.
I blame my boss.
I blame the government.
I blame the school system.
I blame my parents.
I blame the traffic.
I blame myself.

You name it, and we want to blame it. And that gets us nowhere.

That last blame statement I listed—*I blame myself*—may sound appropriate. After all, if you are responsible for your choices and accept each decision you've made has shaped your life, aren't you to blame for your missteps and failures?

Are you responsible for your mistakes? Yes. But let me encourage you to draw a firm line between acknowledging and accepting responsibility for your mistakes and living in a state of blame and regret.

Blaming yourself for your mistakes will not only keep you from moving forward but it can also fill you with paralyzing self-doubt or demoralizing self-loathing.

I'm grateful my dad started teaching me this lesson when I was just a kid. I had poured myself a big glass of orange soda (something we almost never had in the house) and sat down in the den to watch television. I don't remember exactly how it happened or why, but I knocked over the glass. Orange soda spilled all over the floor. My little six-year-old self went into a tailspin of apologizing. I was so upset with myself and probably a little afraid that my dad was going to be mad at me.

I grabbed a towel and tried to mop it up, all the while saying, "I'm sorry. I'm so sorry!"

After about the tenth apology, my dad asked, "Did you mean to do it?"

"Well, no!"

His response still sticks with me. "Then stop apologizing. Accidents happen."

What he didn't say, but I heard loud and clear, was *clean it up and try not to do it again.* It was such a simple lesson, but when I look at my life, I can see how that attitude helped to shape the way I deal with my mistakes. It helped me see that mentally beating myself up over an accident or a mistake solves nothing. Likewise, berating others for their mistakes is not only unhelpful, it also has a detrimental effect on your relationships.

Later in life, *The Traveler's Gift* by Andy Andrews shined a spotlight on how and why to extend an attitude of forgiveness.

I've given away probably a hundred copies of *The Traveler's Gift* because of the way it, and specifically the chapter about forgiveness, impacted me. It helped me understand that forgiveness was a gift I could give to myself. When it comes to forgiving others, I used to think that if someone had wronged me in some way, *they* needed to come and ask for my forgiveness. Until they did, I would hold onto whatever hurt or irritation I felt had been inflicted on me. And then I came across this passage:

> I realize today that it is impossible to fight an enemy living in my head. By forgiving myself, I erase the doubts, fears, and frustration that have kept my past in the present. From this day forward, my history will cease to control my destiny. I have forgiven myself. My life has just begun. I will forgive even those who do not ask for forgiveness. I will forgive those who criticize me unjustly. I will forgive myself. I will greet this day with a forgiving spirit.

Andy's book literally changed the way I think about forgiveness. It helped me see that while I was turning that wrong over in my mind day after day, I was allowing someone else to live rent-free in my head. And at least half the time, that person had no idea I was upset or hurt. I came to understand that forgiving others wasn't something I did only for them; it was something I did for me. The same was true for forgiving myself. That kind of forgiveness was a gift that only I could give myself—and it was a gift I could (and should) give myself every day. I decided, like the character in *The Traveler's Gift*, to begin each day with a forgiving spirit.

So, rather than play the blame game, I work hard to forgive and move on. Moving on includes reflecting on what happened—where things got off track— and taking responsibility to fix what I can. I learn from my mistakes and make adjustments to reduce the chances of them reoccurring. I still make mistakes, a lot of them, in fact. But I try not to make the same mistake twice. Even if I do, forgiveness is the path forward.

Just imagine what your life could be like if blame and guilt were no longer part of it. When you replace unproductive habits and emotions with forgiveness and compassion—with love—for yourself, it will become easier to see the way forward because self-doubt will no longer block your path.

- **What are you waiting for?** When life seems hard, for whatever reason, it's easy to feel stuck. Maybe you're in a stall pattern because you're waiting for an apology. Maybe you're waiting until you feel better, motivated, or confident. Maybe you're waiting until you're absolutely 100 percent sure that your next step is the right one.

    Please, stop waiting. Choose to take responsibility for whatever comes next. You are the *only* one with the power to take the next step.

- **Are you living with resentment or regret?** Do you blame someone or something for your current circumstances? If so, whom do you need to forgive so you can move on? Remember, forgiving someone is not the same as saying, "It's okay." Some wrongs can never be made right. But by choosing to forgive, you are taking control of your life.

- **Have your mistakes and the resulting blame or regret caused you to doubt your abilities, judgment, or worthiness?** Look, we've all made mistakes. Just own up to them, evaluate where and why things went wrong, and then shake off the blame and self-doubt and move forward.

BUILDING CONFIDENCE

The first step of accomplishing anything is to believe that you can do it, and I know that you can do it.

—*Bob Ross*, **painter and host of** *The Joy of Painting* **on PBS**

The difference between taking responsibility and blaming yourself for past mistakes may seem like semantics, but the outcomes are vastly different. Taking responsibility puts you in control. Blaming yourself, as I said before, often leads to self-doubt—which leads nowhere.

Self-doubt stops you from making the decisions you need to make so you can grow and move forward. Even as you are deciding what kind of person you want to be, self-doubt shouts at you:

Who do you think you are that you could have a different life?
You've already screwed up your life, so what's the point?
You've tried before, and things didn't work out.
Putting yourself out there isn't worth the risk.
You're just an imposter—trying to be something you're not.

(By the way, if you hear that last one, chances are you're not an imposter. We'll talk more about that in the next chapter.)

Or maybe that self-doubt will simply affirm criticisms you've heard in the past:

You're getting too big for your britches.
You're never going to amount to anything.
Just keep your head down and do your job.
Stay where you belong.

Don't you want to tell that voice to *get out of your head?*
We've already looked at a few ways to change your thoughts,
but one of the most powerful ways is to take responsibility—
for everything around you—and then *act* in a way that aligns
with your true self, the person you *want* to be.

THE WAY YOU *ACT*
CHANGES THE WAY YOU
THINK. THE WAY YOU
THINK AFFECTS THE WAY
YOU *ACT.* IT'S A CYCLE.
BUT THE GREAT NEWS IS
THAT YOU CAN BREAK
INTO THAT CYCLE AT ANY
POINT AND CHANGE ITS
DIRECTION. YOU CAN
MAKE YOUR THOUGHTS
AND ACTIONS WORK
FOR YOU RATHER THAN
AGAINST YOU.

The way you *act* changes
the way you *think.* The way you
think affects the way you *act.*
It's a cycle. But the great news
is that you can break into that
cycle at any point and change
its direction. You can make
your thoughts and actions work
for you rather than against you.

So we come back to the
heart of this book: **You are the
one who makes the biggest
difference in your life.** Your
thoughts and *actions* determine
your level of happiness, success,
and achievement. You are the deciding factor.

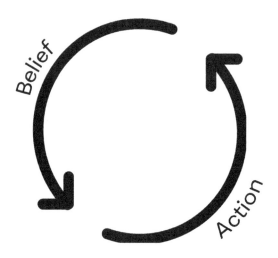

So, where do you start? Start with action. Start by trying. Sure, you may fail at first, but if FAIL stands for *first attempt at learning*, then at least you will be on your way. Fail, learn, grow, try again.

Bob Ross was a master at convincing people to try to paint. For thirty-one seasons (and for several years before launching *The Joy of Painting*), Ross taught people how to pick up the brush, load it with paint, and bring "happy little trees" into view. In almost every painting, even for Ross, there were "happy accidents" to reshape or cover-up. Millions of people watched *The Joy of Painting* on PBS. Before his death, thousands of those viewers sent Ross pictures of the paintings he inspired with his example, calm confidence, and encouragement. While he painted his landscapes, he offered encouragement and often said things like, "People continually say, 'I can't draw a straight line, I don't have a talent, Bob, to do what you do.' That's baloney. Talent is a pursued interest. In other words,

IT'S ALL THE SAME

anything that you're willing to practice, you can do, and this is no exception." [30]

Ross made people *believe* (think) they could paint, and so they did (act). As they saw their own landscapes take shape on the canvas, that belief grew. As much as his television career was about teaching painting, the even more valuable outcome was the *confidence* he instilled in people.

> "**Confidence is a belief in oneself**, the conviction that one has the ability to meet life's challenges and to succeed—**and the willingness to act** accordingly. Being confident requires a realistic sense of one's capabilities and feeling secure in that knowledge." (emphasis added)
> —*Psychology Today*[31]

For a few individuals, confidence is instinctive. For most people, however, it is learned or developed. Confidence builds, as Ross noted of talent, through practice. Try, learn, try again, improve, try again—and again. Building confidence, as with any other skill or muscle, requires effort. It's also developed by realizing that you have the ability to change outcomes—and most notably—to change your life.

Emotional intelligence expert Hendrie Weisinger explains, "The catalyst to bring the function of confidence to life is the realization that your actions influence your results. In other words, 'it's up to you.' If you do not believe in this fully, you will not make efforts to do your best since the outcome is out of your control. . . . Accepting that you can influence

---

[30] Ross, Bob. *Bob Ross: Happy Accidents, Betrayal & Greed.* Netflix Studios. 2021.

[31] Confidence. https://www.psychologytoday.com/us/basics/confidence

the outcome creates a sense of control, and that initiates confidence."[32]

So our cycle expands: Belief —> Confidence —> Action

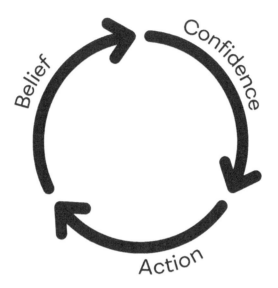

Confidence comes largely through experience, or as Strategic Coach® Founder Dan Sullivan puts it, "Confidence is the reward for making the breakthrough."[33] In other words, confidence follows action. If you're waiting to feel confident before you take action, you will never make a move.

---

[32] Weisinger, Hendrie. "The Essence of Confidence." *Psychology Today. com*. September 1, 2015. https://www.psychologytoday.com/us/ blog/thicken-your-skin/201509/the-essence-confidence.

[33] Sullivan, Dan. "How to Always Increase Your Confidence — Multiplier Mindset." Strategic Coach. YouTube. https://youtu.be/ wBlJ5HbFpYQ.

How: Acknowledge and Celebrate Your Success

Go confidently in the direction of your dreams! Live the life you've imagined.

—Henry David Thoreau

The good news is you already have a history of achievements that you can draw from to increase your confidence. If you're stuck in self-doubt, it may be because you aren't giving yourself the credit you're due. Weisinger notes that confidence increases when people *acknowledge* their successes, however small:

> At one time or another, confident people experienced an event that allowed them to believe "I can do it." An "A" on a test, a big little league hit, getting a part in the school play, a date with a pretty girl or handsome guy—all seem like minuscule events but, in truth, are powerful events because they create feelings of confidence.
>
> Individuals with low confidence can recall a few of these events. This does not mean they did not have successful experiences when growing up. More likely, it means that they did not pay attention to their successes. Confident people developed themselves by noting and often celebrating their micro successes and used them, probably subconsciously, to create positive expectations for more successful experiences. This experience is the root of the confidence-building statement, "I did it once before; I can do it again."

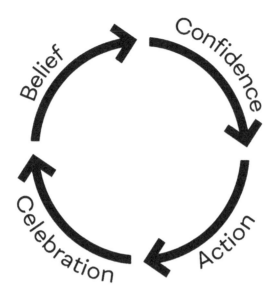

The successes that build confidence can seem insignificant, and sometimes they *are*, as Weisinger pointed out. But sometimes, as author and entrepreneur Derek Sivers has explained, the things that are simple, easy, or obvious to you are unique, seemingly impossible, or amazing to others.[34] Your superpower, remember, often comes naturally.

If someone asked you to share your success story, you may think, *What success story? I'm just doing what I do.* What you've already accomplished may seem like no big deal to you. Those achievements, however, might actually be the stepping stones to your next big goal. Recognizing those accomplishments—celebrating and then reverse engineering them—will keep you in forward motion.

If you can't explain how you've gotten this far in your life or career, you're not alone. People don't always know how

---

[34] Sivers, Derek. "Obvious to you. Amazing to others." November 21, 2010. https://sive.rs/obvious.

they achieved their success, and thus, they don't know how to leverage it into future successes. Dan Sullivan offers a model he calls the Four C's for building the kind of confidence that propels your growth, and an essential part of the process is reflecting on your previous achievements.

DAN SULLIVAN'S FOUR C'S[35]

1. **Commitment**—Decide what you want to do (or who you want to be) and *commit* to making that happen. You may not know *how* to accomplish that dream or goal yet. That's okay. The first step is to commit.

2. **Courage**—The next step is to decide that you are going to move forward with the courage to figure out what needs to be done, the courage to change, the courage to stay the course.

3. **Capability**—With your commitment and courage secure, the next step is to develop the capability. Remember: Try, Fail, Learn, Grow. Try again.

4. **Confidence**—The result or "reward" of committing to yourself or your goal, living with the courage to pursue it to the end, and developing the capability that proves you *can* succeed culminates with the fourth C: Confidence.

Making that initial commitment can feel terrifying. With no assurances for success, that nagging voice in your head will offer up all sorts of reasons why you shouldn't go after your

---

[35] Sullivan, Dan. "How to Always Increase Your Confidence — Multiplier Mindset." Strategic Coach. YouTube. https://youtu.be/wBlJ5HbFpYQ

dreams. One way to quiet those fears, Sullivan explains, is to reflect on times when you've acted with courage and succeeded. Paying attention to and learning from previous achievements provides proof, or at least reassurance, that you can develop the capability to grow.

And this is where I'll add one more C to the list.

DAVID'S 5TH C

5. **Celebrate**—Acknowledge and *celebrate* your wins. You have survived every challenge you've ever faced and every trauma or drama that has ever come into your life. If you need evidence of that, just look in the mirror. You're still here, making plans for your future. Celebrate that! Remind yourself that you are strong enough, good enough, and *courageous* enough to push through whatever fears or obstacles you may encounter along the way. And then do it. Whatever *it* is that will move you in the direction of your dreams.

  - **What are your talents or superpowers?** What comes so easily that you tend to discount its significance?

  - **What have you accomplished?** No matter who you are or what your background is, you *have* experienced wins. What are they? What skills have you developed because of the challenges you've faced?

  - **Reflect on a time when you acted despite fear or doubt.** What motivated you to try and to keep going? What can you take from that experience and apply to your current goals or circumstances?

As much as I want to encourage you, I also want you to have the right expectations. No matter how confident you are, you won't always succeed. You will experience failures. Sometimes, a blob of blue paint will drop right in the middle of your green forest. The question is this: What are you going to do when things don't go your way? Even if it doesn't feel like a "happy accident," I hope you will find a way to turn that blue blob into something beautiful.

Remember, this is *your* life. It bears repeating that it is always your responsibility to respond to challenges, discouragement, pain, and even the worst circumstances with courage, kindness, and compassion toward yourself first. Yes, *first*. It isn't selfish to do so. Forgiving yourself empowers you to forgive others. Being kind and compassionate toward yourself gives you the courage to risk making mistakes. You'll be free to pick yourself up and accept responsibility while casting off blame. Feeling lighter and stronger, you'll be able to move forward with the confidence that *you* are worthy of *your* best.

5

YOU CAN CHOOSE TO BE UNSTOPPABLE

We ask ourselves, Who am I to be brilliant, gorgeous, talented, fabulous? Actually, who are you not to be? You are a child of God. Your playing small doesn't serve the world.

—Marian Williamson

"What does this passage mean?"

I was sitting in Mrs. Schultz's honors English class in my junior year of high school. We were going over our reading assignment when she read a few lines from the book and then asked that question.

An answer immediately popped into my mind. I thought about raising my hand, but when I looked around, I saw that no one else's hand was up. So I sat there. I was sure everyone in the class was smarter than I was. If they didn't know the answer, my answer had to be wrong. Mrs. Schultz called on a few of my classmates. Student after student offered their guesses, but the teacher shook her head at each one. With every wrong answer, my confidence sank. *If they aren't getting it right, there's no chance I'm right,* I thought.

Finally, my friend Allan raised his hand and gave the teacher the right answer—*my* answer. The answer I'd come up with as soon as the teacher asked the question. I had been right all along, but what I believed about myself—that I wasn't as smart as my peers—stopped me from putting myself out there with an answer.

When I first considered writing this book, one thought played on repeat in my mind: *Who am I to tell anyone that I know the answer?*

Self-doubt never fails to speak up.

Sure, I've experienced some success both personally and professionally. I'm happy with my life, my relationships, and my career, but I'm not a success coach. More to the point, I don't *want* to be a coach—success, life, business, or otherwise.

So why did I go through with this book? My life is good, safe, and comfortable. Why am I raising my head above the tall grass of my simple, satisfying life and risking it being chopped off by people who may know more than me—or, more likely, by naysayers who know nothing except how to bring others down?

Because I *do* know the answer.

I know how to create a great life.

I know there are no limitations except the ones you put on yourself.

I know *you* are your best chance, your best option, your best advocate.

Knowing the truth and not sharing it seemed more dangerous than putting myself out there and doing something that could help others.

The idea of not helping you—when I *know* I can—felt scary. It felt wrong.

So here I am, trusting you and the rest of the world to not lop off my head.

Imposter syndrome, that feeling of *Who am I to be the one to do this?* was a potential roadblock for me even writing this book. It's a feeling of insecurity that people have dealt with (or succumbed to) for ages. Maybe you have too.

I recognized it because I'd come up against it more than a few times in my life. One of the first times I became aware of its effect (even though I didn't know just what to label the feeling) happened in Mrs. Schultz's class.

By the time I'd reached college, I'd gained a little more confidence. Not complete confidence, but at least enough to evaluate and question ideas presented by others if they didn't align with my own way of thinking. Or maybe that's just part of being a young adult. Regardless, I remember reading *How to Win Friends and Influence People* by Dale Carnegie in preparation for my summer job as a camp counselor. It's a fantastic book, of course, and the camp director required all the staff members to read it. Most of it resonated, but when I came to a part about not speaking your mind—or at least not the first ideas that come to mind—I paused. *My first thought is usually pretty darn good*, I thought. No, I didn't (and still don't) say the right thing 100 percent of the time. I know I've said dumb or awkward things now and then, even as an adult. But I had learned by then to believe in myself enough to speak up. If I needed to go back and amend something I said, well, that was okay too. These days, my goal is to live in a way that builds up the kind of goodwill with people that allows them to give me the benefit of the doubt so that when I don't say exactly the right thing, those around me know that my intention is not to harm or offend.

I knew that, for me, stopping to deeply question every thought before letting it loose in the world was a sure way to *not* be myself. Looking back from a more experienced and compassionate perspective, I realize that people teach what they need (or needed) to learn. That is certainly true about so much of what ended up in this book. I'm sharing lessons I had to learn because I know I'm not alone in my struggles. I also know that you may have already learned a few of these lessons yourself. That's great. Do what I did with Carnegie's book and take what you need to move forward on your journey and let the rest serve as a reminder on an as-needed basis. Because as my opening comments of this chapter proved, we all need to be reminded of the truth when feelings like imposter syndrome, fear, and other roadblocks block the path.

Most of the time, I am able to keep imposter syndrome in check by controlling the voice in my head. (See Chapter 3.) Every once in a while, though, especially when I'm considering doing something bigger and bolder—like writing a book—I need to go back and read my own advice.

Imposter syndrome is only one of the many roadblocks you may come across. Perfectionism, fear, and a lack of discipline are a few others that have the potential to stop you from doing what you need to do to become who you want to be. As with everything else we've talked about thus far, you have a choice in how to deal with those roadblocks. I hope you'll choose to break through them and become *unstoppable*.

ROADBLOCK: PERFECTIONISM

Feeling the need to be perfect doesn't make you perfect. It just makes you paralyzed. So let go of that because you're not going to be perfect. And if you're very lucky, you'll learn to be yourself.

—David Sedaris

Even before he was commissioned to sculpt *David*, Michelangelo had earned the status of being one of the greatest artists of his time. Then, before he reached the ripe old age of thirty, he had created what remains one of the world's most renowned works of art.

Imagine the weight of success that Michelangelo might have felt and what it could have been like to have the incredible Leonardo da Vinci as his main competitor.

Did he fear that one botched commission would mean the end of his career? That rather than being known as an artistic genius, with one flop, he would become someone who was once great but had lost his edge—a washed-up has-been before turning forty.

If he wasn't a perfectionist before then (which he might well have been), Michelangelo certainly became one in the years that followed. The trait led to new and incredible work, including the painting of the Sistine Chapel's ceiling that still draws tourists today, but it came with a cost. His demanding and exacting behavior left him with few friends and fewer assistants (because he fired them on a whim). It's also believed to be the reason he tried to destroy the *Florentine Pieta* (also known as *The Deposition*), a sculpture he had worked on for eight years. The theories are that his frustration with flaws in the marble, an irritating assistant, or what he saw as a problem with his work sent him into a rage. He picked up a sledgehammer and wailed on what some thought would be one of his greatest accomplishments.

Everyone who had seen the piece marveled at it. But to Michelangelo, it wasn't good enough. Nothing but perfection could ever be.

Success, or the fear of losing it, is one factor that can drive people to demand perfection of themselves and others. When you've reached the top, falling can be unthinkable. If you're a perfectionist, each success raises the stakes. Every new opportunity is a chance to beat your best or to fail miserably.

Although some people point to genetics, perfectionism is often a learned behavior caused by any combination of these potential factors:

- Rigid, high parental expectations

- Highly critical, shaming, or abusive parents

- Excessive praise for your achievements

- Low self-esteem or feeling inadequate

- Believing your self-worth is determined by your achievements

- Black-and-white thinking

- Efforts to feel in control

- Cultural expectations[36]

For perfectionists, there is no middle ground or *good enough*. Life—all of it—is all or nothing. Failure, however minor, is often viewed as a character flaw.

If you're thinking, *What's so bad about wanting things to be perfect?* Take it as a warning sign that perfectionism may be a roadblock for you

Study after study has shown that demanding perfection from yourself, your work, or others can put you on the path not only for inevitable disappointment but for everything from depression and anxiety to burnout.[37] Perfectionism can wreck

---

[36] Martin, Sharon. "What Causes Perfectionism?" *PsychCentral* December 8, 2015. https://psychcentral.com/blog/imperfect/2015/12/what-causes-perfectionism#1.

[37] Ibid.

your self-esteem and your self-confidence. And they're different. Your self-esteem is the way you feel about yourself—think about the way you talk to yourself (Chapter 3). Self-confidence goes back to what we talked about in Chapter 4—your belief in your abilities and judgment. As it did for much of Michelangelo's life, a complete unwillingness to compromise can alienate people and damage or even destroy relationships.

Perfectionism pushes people to accept nothing less than their very best, a strategy that can backfire. "Perfectionists often end up achieving much less than they aspire to because they hold back, procrastinate, and even stop taking on challenges altogether—because it's better to not have entered the race than to have spun out in ignominy," says Tracy Dennis-Tiwary, a psychology and neuroscience professor and author of *Future Tense*.[38] Perfectionists are also famous for their indecisiveness. (The search for the perfect couch lasted the better part of a decade for Steve Jobs and his wife, Laurene Powell Jobs.)[39]

Ironically, perfectionism tends to lead to less-than-perfect results. "Perfectionists counterintuitively turn out lower-quality work than they're actually capable of doing. Perfectionists take longer than non-perfectionists on repetitive or boring tasks, create more inaccuracies, and work less efficiently," Dennis-Tiwary explains. The reason? They tend to spend too much time focusing on every detail, and fatigue or familiarity takes over. When that happens, the quality of their work suffers.

[38] Dennis-Tiwary, Tracy. "Perfectionists: Lowering your standards can improve your mental health." *The Washington Post*. October 19, 2022. https://www.washingtonpost.com/wellness/2022/10/19/perfectionism-anxiety-excellence.

[39] Canales, Katie. "Laurene Powell Jobs says it took her and detail-obsessed husband Steve Jobs 8 years to buy a couch because they couldn't agree on one." *Insider*. September 8, 2022. https://www.businessinsider.com/laurene-powell-jobs-steve-jobs-8-years-with-no-couch-2022-9.

Sometimes, that focus on the details is a delay tactic. My friend Sam Horn, author of *Someday Is Not a Day of the Week,* says, "Perfectionism is a form of procrastination." She works with best-selling authors and knows from experience that "If we try to get it right, we won't get it written because trying to get it perfect is an exercise in futility."[40]

Creativity is another victim of perfectionism. Research shows that the rigid focus of perfection can stifle outside-the-box thinking.[41]

Here's the good news: If you can learn to be a perfectionist, you have proved that you are capable of learning to adjust your standards—which means you can lower them. More good news? You can still have big goals and high standards without being a perfectionist. Patrick Gaudreau, a professor of psychology at the University of Ottawa, calls for *excellencism* rather than perfectionism.

In the creativity study referenced above, Gaudreau and his fellow researchers found that when people pursue excellence rather than perfection, it opens the door to "divergent thinking."[42]

---

[40] Horn, Sam. "Did You Know PERFECTIONISM is a Form of PROCRASTINATION?" LinkedIn. https://www.linkedin.com/pulse/perfectionism-just-another-word-procrastination-sam-horn/. October 21, 2017.

[41] Goulet-Pelletier, Jean-Christophe, Patrick Gaudreau, Denis Cousineau. "Is perfectionism a killer of creative thinking? A test of the model of excellencism and perfectionism." *British Journal of Psychology.* Vol. 113, Issue 1. February 2022. Pages 1-1v, 1-352. https://bpspsychub.onlinelibrary.wiley.com/doi/epdf/10.1111/bjop.12530.

[42] Smith, Martin M., Simon B. Sherry, Vanja Vidovic, Paul L. Hewitt, Gordon L. Flett. "Does perfectionism confer risk for depressive symptoms? A meta-analytic test of the mediating role of stress and social disconnection." *Journal of Research in Personality,* Volume 86, 2020. https://doi.org/10.1016/j.jrp.2020.103954.

"Excellence can be attained without reaching perfection," the researchers explain. And that excellence is satisfying and a feeling perfectionists rarely experience because of their impossible standards and tendency to beat themselves up falling short. Perfect is the enemy of good. If you're waiting to launch something new, Coach Dan Sullivan's advice is to get your project or product to the 80-percent done mark as quickly as possible. "In many situations in life, just doing 80 percent the first time is good enough," Dan explains. "People who are perfectionists, of course, would never accept this. They keep working on the project, making endless improvements until it is 'perfect'—even though none of this extra work is necessary. This has nothing to do with the project itself or its usefulness to other people. It only has to do with what is going on inside of the perfectionist's mind."[43]

Eliminate the kind of procrastination that comes from perfectionism. You can figure out the other 20 percent *if*, in fact, you need to do so. Regardless of why you feel the need to be perfect, focusing on excellence rather than perfection can lead to more enjoyment of the task, better quality of work, and less self-criticism. Let good enough be good enough.

ROADBLOCK: FEAR

Sometimes the byproduct of a preposterous goal is better than reaching it.

—Steve Sims

---

[43] Sullivan, Dan. *The 80% Approach.* Strategic Coach. Toronto, Canada: Strategic Coach. 2018.

Setting outrageous, impossible, or seemingly unachievable goals sounds like a sure plan for failure. Why would you set a goal that you *knew* you couldn't achieve?

Truth is, most people wouldn't. Most people would set reasonable goals and maybe a *stretch* goal or two but nothing so crazy that there's no way to achieve it.

Steve Sims is not most people. He's one of those guys who believes that the impossible means it might just take a little longer. The former bricklayer from the south side of London is a bestselling author, consultant, and the "visionary founder of the world's first luxury concierge that delivers the highest level of personalized travel, transportation, and cutting-edge entertainment services to corporate executives, celebrities, professional athletes, and other discerning individuals interested in living life to its fullest."[44] That's a comprehensive job description and one that took time and plenty of mistakes and outright failures to create for himself. Judging from his high-octane life and the list of happy clients and the outrageous experiences he's orchestrated, those failures were worth it.

It's no surprise that Sims set impossible goals, but he doesn't do it because he wants to fail. Those impossible goals are the key to even greater results:

> If you have a goal to make $2 million this year, and you think that's a ridiculous, sexy, crazy goal, then you need to make it $10 million. Fail, and you achieve $5 million.
>
> You see, goals are target points. I hate to say it, but most of the time we don't actually hit our goal. We fall slightly short. . . . We live in an imperfect world, so most goals are not fully achieved.

---

[44] https://www.stevedsims.com/

I'm a great believer that if you know that not all goals are achieved, then you need to make your goals stupid, ridiculous, and laughable.

You want to be 180 pounds, so make your goal 170. If you fail, you'll still be at 175 pounds. You want a house on a beach but fail, yet you still get a house that's within walking distance of the ocean. In order to achieve what you want, you have to aim for what is stupid.[45]

The idea of setting a goal with the expectation that failure is not just possible but almost assured might not sound particularly fun or exciting. It may even sound terrifying. But why does failure scare us so much?

Research shows that humans are born with only two fears: the fear of falling and the fear of loud sounds.[46] Somewhere along the way, we pick up other fears, learning them from the people around us and from our environment. If your mother was terrified of bees, you may run for cover when you see one. Maybe seeing one of the *Jaws* movies turned you off from ever SCUBA diving or from the ocean altogether. Spiders and sharks aren't things you knew to fear when you were born. Those are learned fears.

Similarly, we aren't born with the fear of failure. We learned it from our parents, teachers, peers, our success culture, and from experience. It isn't failure that we fear, though. The real fear is shame.

Shame is a feeling humans avoid, sometimes to the detriment of their true potential. The fear of failure isn't necessarily

45 Sims, Steve D. *Go for Stupid.* House of Nomad SOC. 2022.
46 Kounang, Nadia. "What is the science behind fear?" CNN.com. October 29, 2015. cnn.com/2015/10/29/health/science-of-fear/index.html.

about being disappointed to have missed a goal or made a mistake that no one but you will ever know about. (Although if you're a perfectionist, you're probably harder on yourself than anyone else ever would be.) The fear of failure, often, is rooted in the desire to avoid being rejected, publicly embarrassed, or judged by others. Interestingly, the desire to avoid judgment can also be at the core of the fear of success.

FEAR OF SUCCESS

Procrastination is the fear of success. People procrastinate because they are afraid of the success that they know will result if they move ahead now. Because success is heavy, carries a responsibility with it, it is much easier to procrastinate and live on the "someday I'll" philosophy.

—Denis Waitley

Success is exactly what you want, right?

Success means you would get what you want, finally achieve a goal, overcome a bad habit, or climb out of a place you no longer want to be.

Success sounds perfect—except for the consequences:

- To succeed, you'll have to put in even more work, energy, and effort—and you may fear you'll have to maintain that level of intensity for the long haul.

- If you succeed, people will expect *more* from you. The demands will increase, and you may fear you won't be able to keep up.

- You may fear that if you succeed, your achievements will keep someone else from getting what they want.

- And what happens when your family and friends reject you because they believe you think you're too good for them? No one wants to be ostracized by family members or close friends.

For some people, playing small, giving up right before crossing the finish line, or not trying at all feels safer than dealing with how others will respond to their success. You might think, *I would never!* But hang on. Have you ever given up on a big dream because it would mean *everything* in your life would have to change? Have you ever opted not to apply for a promotion or gig because you knew a friend or colleague wanted the same job? Have you ever kept a personal win or talent to yourself because you didn't want to make someone feel bad?

Most of us have, perhaps without realizing the motive behind our actions. That's what makes the fear of success so tricky. You aren't always aware that you are sabotaging your chances of success or standing in your own way.

Fear of Being Laughed At

You wouldn't worry so much about what others think of you if you realized how seldom they do.

—Eleanor Roosevelt

Sims adds one more fear to the list: "Today, we're in a world where people are terrified, not of failing, but of people laughing at them." In other words, we tend to put too much stock into what people think of us.

In what Sims calls our "gotcha culture," it's common for people to laugh when others fail. Think about what you laughed at most when watching *America's Funniest Home Videos*. It was probably some dare-devil dude tumbling through the air and landing face-first in the mud after attempting some crazy feat. He failed so spectacularly that someone thought the video had a shot at the $10,000 prize—because it would make people laugh.

This fear of being ridiculed is what makes people look around after a fall (literally or figuratively). *Did anyone see me? Did anyone film it? Is anyone laughing?* It's also the reason that some companies, like Microsoft and Google, create space and time in employees' schedules where they have the freedom to try new things when no one is watching. These companies and others know that when people have the freedom to try out new—even *stupid*—ideas without fear of being laughed at, genius often rises to the surface.

WHAT ARE YOU
AFRAID OF?

All of these fears—the fear of failure, success, and being humiliated—are potential roadblocks. *Potential* in that you don't have to allow them to stop you. If you find yourself procrastinating on the things you want most in life or throwing up a wall of defensiveness or defeat, ask yourself these questions:

- What am I afraid of *and why*?

- What's the worst that could happen if I fail?

- What's the *most likely* thing to happen?

- What's the best thing that could happen if I succeed? Isn't that worth a shot?

ROADBLOCK: DISCIPLINE (OR A LACK THEREOF)

If you want to transform your life in a positive way, that transformation will not happen by itself. You need to make it happen.

—*Jocko Willink*

There's a reason one of the most repeated phrases in a dieter's life is "I'll start again tomorrow." It leaves today wide open for another serving of dessert, fried chicken, or deep-dish Chicago-style pizza.

And when tomorrow comes, well, there's always another tomorrow.

You can have the best intentions and set important goals for yourself—goals you really care about, like reading a smaller number on the scale, having a bigger number in the bank account, spending more time with the people who matter most, improving your health, launching a business, or learning a new skill to advance your career. But without discipline *today,* you're more likely to abandon those goals than to see them through.

Willpower. Self-Control. Self-Restraint. *Self-Discipline.*

None of those words sound as fun as doing whatever the heck you want, but as *Atomic Habits* author James Clear points out, "Success usually comes down to choosing the pain of discipline over the ease of distraction."[47] And that requires willpower.

The trouble is that willpower is fickle. It can be swayed or incinerated by something as simple as the impulse purchase

---

[47] Clear, James. "Willpower." JamesClear.com. https://jamesclear.com/willpower/.

rack in the checkout lane at the grocery store, the sound of the ice cream truck rolling through in the neighborhood, or that BOGO sale on your favorite *anything*. When we are tired, hungry, or in a bad mood—or even a great one—we are at risk of our self-discipline taking a nosedive.

So, what's the answer? The cure for weak willpower?

It depends on who you ask.

- Some experts say the best course of action is to give yourself grace when you give in to the desire for instant gratification. Expect that it's going to happen from time to time and accept it. There's no point in beating yourself up. Making yourself feel bad for slipping up is counterproductive.

- James Clear cites other experts who say the key to strengthening your self-discipline muscles is temptation bundling—combining tasks you don't like to do (exercise, for example) with activities you enjoy (like listening to your favorite podcast). "Temptation bundling offers a simple way to accomplish these tasks that are always important but never feel urgent. By using your guilty pleasures to pull you in, you make it easier to follow through on more difficult habits that pay off in the long-run."[48]

- Other experts on the subject, such as Jocko Willink, a retired Navy SEAL, leadership consultant, and bestselling author, have little patience for wiggle room or whining about how hard it is to be disciplined. "You have control over your mind. You just have to assert it," Willink says. "You have to decide

---

[48] Clear, James. *Atomic Habits.* Penguin Random House: New York. 2018.

that you are going to be in control, that you are going to do what YOU want [or need] to do."[49] It doesn't matter how you feel; you do the thing—rain or shine, happy or sad, tired or frustrated, weak or lazy.

Different experts. Different approaches. Which approach is the right one? *The right one is the one that works for you.* You are the one who knows yourself best.

If being gentle with yourself motivates you to improve, show yourself some compassion and give yourself latitude.

If you respond better to strict goals and unyielding effort, well then, as Willink says, "next time you are feeling weak or lazy or soft or emotional, tell those feelings they don't get a vote. You are declaring martial law on your mind: Mind Control."

Or maybe you know you are most likely to succeed with intentional strategies like temptation bundling. Great. Make a plan and stick to it. And if you slip, get back on track the same day. (You might want to prepare a plan for that too.)

My point is this: *You* set the goals. *You* determine your path and parameters. *You* can choose the long way or the most direct route, but *you* are responsible for traveling it. No one else can do it for you. What matters most is the person you become along the way.

I'll leave you with this thought from Willink's book *Discipline Equals Freedom* because it echoes the truth that *you* are the one who can turn the roadblock of discipline into a ramp to achieving your goals:

---

[49] Willink, Jocko. *Discipline Equals Freedom.* St. Martin's Press: New York.

Discipline comes from within. Discipline is an internal force. Sure, you can have discipline imposed on you by a person, like a drill instructor or that self-help guru on TV, but the reality is: He won't give you discipline. Because that external discipline is not strong. It will not survive. It cannot stand on its own.

What you're looking for, what you need, is **SELF-DISCIPLINE.**[50]

And what I will tell you is that *what you need is you.* You are the answer. Now, you just have to believe it.

How: Meditation and Emotional Freedom Technique

Your calm mind is the ultimate weapon against your challenges. So relax.

—Bryant McGill

The roadblocks of imposter syndrome, perfectionism, fear, and a lack of discipline have different definitions, but they can create similar symptoms: avoidance, anxiety, stress, and a feeling of being out of control. Left unchecked, they can cause debilitating panic attacks and depression.

Many of the tools and techniques discussed in previous chapters, including visualization, NLP, and reminding yourself of previous successes, can help you change the way you think about these roadblocks so you can break through them. Those tools are great for the long term. But when your blood pressure is rising because you're stressed, or you're on the verge

---

[50] Willink, Jocko. *Discipline Equals Freedom.* St. Martin's Press: New York.

of a panic attack because you are afraid of failing others (or yourself), you need strategies that offer quick, calming results.

That's where meditation and the Emotional Freedom Technique (EFT) come in. You can use either or both whenever you need to bring down your heart rate, calm your nerves, and stem the flood of negative thoughts.

MEDITATION

I'm a firm believer that if you don't control your thoughts, your thoughts will control you. Meditation is one technique that can help you direct your thoughts when it feels that they are coming like a tidal wave.

For many years, the word *meditation* conjured images of eccentric yogis sitting on a mountaintop in the lotus position for hours on end. If that's your impression of meditation, it's time for an update. The centuries-old practice has become mainstream in the past couple of decades and is used today by everyone from elementary school students to entrepreneurs to celebrities. It's a quick and simple way to bring calm to chaos.

One common misconception about meditation is that it's too difficult. As one stressed-out friend complained: "I can't just make my brain stop."

Agreed. You can't make your brain stop. (That's called being dead.) You can't *not* have a thought. But you can use simple techniques to break a pattern of anxious thoughts.

Another misconception is that it takes too long. That same friend told me he didn't have time to meditate. What he didn't understand is how just a few minutes of meditation can create a calming effect. Those few minutes a day can also increase the brain's ability to focus. Meditation isn't something you do to the exclusion of daily life. It's a tool that helps you function in the active world. Research studies show that as few as five minutes of meditation in the morning can be a beneficial way to start the day. Twenty minutes of quiet or guided meditation can bring down your stress and anxiety levels after an argument or during an especially intense day.[51]

Simply sitting still in a comfortable position for a few minutes and taking slow, deep breaths is helpful. If your thoughts are in overdrive, using a mantra—a word or phrase of your choosing—can help focus your attention and quiet your mind. When a stray thought comes to mind, acknowledge it and return to your mantra.

There are countless resources for learning how to meditate, including apps like Declutter The Mind, Calm, Headspace, and FitMind, which offer guided meditations, soothing music, and simple timers to keep you from thinking about the clock. (The timer will also wake you if you fall asleep while meditating. Hey, it happens!)

EMOTIONAL FREEDOM TECHNIQUE

The Emotional Freedom Technique, also known as *tapping*, draws on the principles of acupressure and psychology to quickly calm the mind and body. It seems too simple to be effective, but clinical studies have validated the method and regular people who've tried it swear by the nerve-calming results. A review of studies published in the *Journal of Clinical Psychology* found that EFT was associated with significant improvements in symptoms of anxiety and depression, as well as reductions in cortisol, a hormone related to stress.[52]

---

[51] Murphy, Amber. "How long should you meditate for?" *Declutter the Mind.* https://declutterthemind.com/blog/how-long-should-you-meditate-for.

[52] "Emotional Freedom Techniques (EFT) for Anxiety and Depression: A Systematic Review." Journal of Clinical Psychology, vol. 72, no. 7, 2016, pp. 576-588. https://onlinelibrary.wiley.com/doi/abs/10.1002/cpp.1938

Nick Ortner, author of *The Tapping Solution* and co-founder of a company by the same name, explains that EFT is called *tapping* because that's exactly what it is. Using your fingers, you lightly tap on the endpoints of the meridians of your body.

The tapping points are the

- top of the head

- side of the hand (karate chop point)

- eyebrows

- side of the eyes

- under the eye

- under the nose

- chin

- collar bone

- under the arm

Nick's sister and business partner Jessica Ortner, author of *The Tapping Solution for Weight Loss and Body Confidence,* explains the process for tapping in a quick video on *TheTappingSolution.com.*[53] (And, yes, there's an app for that.) In a nutshell, you begin by focusing on the source of your stress. With the issue in focus, you start tapping while repeating a phrase that allows you to release that stress. You might say something like, "Even though I'm feeling stressed about this deadline, I accept how I feel, and I give myself permission to relax."

From there, you acknowledge how you feel as you tap a few times on each tapping point. When you feel better or a

---

[53] https://www.thetappingsolution.com/

little less anxious, you continue tapping while speaking a few positive phases. You might say something like, "I feel calm and confident," or "I am prepared."

So why does tapping work? Because the mind and body are connected. "When we feel stressed, we don't just feel that stress in our head, we feel it with our whole body," Jessica explains.[54] Incorporating a physical action with a mental process allows the body to calm down and shift the way the situation you're facing affects you.

Both meditation and EFT are effective and simple to practice. Add them to your toolbox and try one or both the next time you hit a roadblock.

---

[54] Ortner, Jessica. "How to Tap with Jessica Ortner." YouTube. https://youtu.be/BPqGjcxoPS8.

6

YOU DON'T HAVE TO GO IT ALONE

Once we recognize the fact that every individual is a treasury of hidden and unsuspected qualities, our lives become richer, our judgment better, and our world is more right. It is not love that is blind, it is only the unnoticing eye that cannot see the real qualities of people.

— *Charles H. Percy*

I've been called a "serial co-founder," and the title fits. Much of the success I've had in business has come from partnerships. I learned early on that the best and brightest people often work in teams. That wisdom came *after* my first and least viable enterprise as a commission-only real estate agent. Being a solopreneur, at least for me, was hard, lonely, and frustrating. So, my next venture was with a friend who needed a partner to execute his idea to create a staffing company. I knew just enough about staffing to be dangerous, but

I figured things out along the way. Our successful company grew and eventually served clients nationwide.

My subsequent entrepreneurial endeavors have had a similar origin story. I partner with people to execute great ideas. It's rewarding to see those ideas come to fruition, so much so that for the past seven years, I've worn a MyIntent bracelet with the word "Empower." It's my mantra. Les Brown has said that the most expensive real estate in the world is the cemetery because that's where all the ideas that never got executed are dead forever. My intent to empower others by partnering with them has prevented at least a few great ideas from dying.

Throughout this book, we've talked about you and the fact that you are the one in control of your life and happiness. You know by now that no one is going to save the day for you. You have to do that for yourself. You have to be the one to take action.

And that's true. Your success, in whatever form or fashion, starts with you.

But that doesn't mean that you have to do life alone.

Steve Jobs had Steve Wozniak.

Sherlock had Holmes.

Lucy had Ethel.

Even the Lone Ranger had Tonto.

We need partners, mentors, coaches, and cheerleaders. We need people who are brave enough to challenge us and are committed to bringing out the best in us.

You are surrounded by people who can help you and want to see you succeed. You may not even know some of those people—yet. You still need to meet them. Connect with them. That's what this chapter is about: the relationships that help us grow *and* how to grow those relationships.

MAKE THE FIRST MOVE

Saying hello doesn't have an ROI. It's about building relationships.

—Gary Vaynerchuk

The nature of news media is that much of the time it highlights what's wrong with the world: the worst of humanity, local and global catastrophes, conflict and crisis, and all of the differences that divide us. We see and hear these reports *because* we stop and pay attention to them. In turn, advertisers pay the outlets for our attention. To keep the money rolling in, the media amps up our exposure to the world's drama to hold our attention until, as Brandon Stanton explains, "The news we hear is largely a reflection of what we find interesting as opposed to a representative reflection of the world in general."[55]

Stanton is the creator of Humans of New York (HONY), which he started in 2010 as a personal photography project. He didn't own a television when he moved to New York, so unencumbered by nightly news reports of gang violence, muggings, and murders, Stanton wandered into boroughs and neighborhoods that more informed people intentionally avoid. A struggling artist, he was on a mission to photograph 10,000 New Yorkers and create a visual, humanized map of the city. "I stopped thousands of people in every neighborhood in New York, and everybody was pretty nice," he said in a TEDx talk in 2012. "And you know, that's pretty amazing given New

[55] Stanton, Brandon. "Brandon Stanton: The Good Story." TEDx Columbia College. November 2012. https://www.youtube.com/watch?v=HGzgyVAlsDE&t=585s&ab_channel=TEDxColumbiaCollege.

York's reputation as being a very dangerous city—one where you keep to yourself and don't talk to strangers."[56]

The experience gave him a different perspective of people and of the city itself than the news or Netflix portrays. Perceptions of some of those neighborhoods—of violence, danger, and conflict—weren't what he experienced. Instead, he saw people working to make ends meet, children playing in the streets, couples sitting on park benches, people perching on stoops, and homeless men and women struggling to stay warm.

In his TEDx talk, he shared an image of a group of tough guys—guys you might cross the street to avoid. He didn't. He stopped to talk with them and asked to take their photo, and they agreed. And try as they might to look like thugs for the camera, they had a hard time keeping a straight face when Stanton accidentally stepped into the spray of an open fire hydrant as he moved into position for the shot.

"We are presented with a world that is more violent, more dangerous, and more sexy than the one we actually live in," he pointed out. "The world outside your window isn't nearly as dangerous or violent or as sexy as the world inside the TV." To the contrary, he said, "It's still filled with people that have very interesting stories. They're just not always exciting enough to make your local news."

What began in 2010 as a personal project in New York City has turned into a community bonding experience on a global scale. As *CBS Sunday Morning* correspondent Jim Axelrod said to Brandon Stanton during an interview in 2020, "You shrink the world."[57] His images close the gap between

---

56   Ibid.
57   "Humans": Connecting with the world one photo at a time. *CBS Sunday Morning.* December 13, 2020. https://www.youtube.com/watch?v=eSUDUbk2rf4&ab_channel=CBSSundayMorning.

perception and everyday life. They show that regardless of race, money, culture, or career, people are people.

Stanton wasn't very far into the project when he decided he wanted to do more than capture images. He wanted to get to know the people he photographed—and he wanted to share their stories. Gently breaking down people's barriers to get to those stories, Stanton now asks questions that might seem too personal in any other setting. He doesn't want trite answers. He wants to hear something he hasn't heard before, something unique to the individual. Unlike someone's philosophy on life, which might be very similar to a thousand other people's ideas about what's right or wrong, good or bad, "All of our stories are our own," he explained to a group of University College Dublin students when he visited the campus to accept the school's James Joyce award.[58] As the camera clicks, he asks questions like, "What's your greatest struggle right now?" And amazingly, people tell him things they may have never told anyone else.

THE POWER OF CONNECTION

Connection is why we're here; it is what gives purpose and meaning to our lives.

—Brené Brown, **Daring Greatly**

The connection those stories created, from New York or New Delhi, propelled Humans of New York (HONY) from a photography blog into a series of bestselling books and a

---

[58] Stanton, Brandon. "On how I approach strangers in the street | Humans of New York creator Brandon Stanton | UCD, Dublin." YouTube. April 24, 2014. https://www.youtube.com/watch?v= KPxzlGPrM3A&ab_channel=UCD-UniversityCollegeDublin.

docuseries produced by Facebook. "It wasn't necessarily the photography itself that was interesting people; it was meeting a stranger," Stanton said during the *CBS Sunday Morning* interview.[59] The unfiltered honesty of the images and stories people share—stories of doubt, fear, challenge, happiness, and most of all, pain—fosters a feeling of connection across physical and socioeconomic boundaries.

I'm sure people share their stories with Stanton for all sorts of reasons. The most obvious reason is that he *asks* to hear their story and then lets them talk. Using his listening and storytelling superpowers for good, Stanton has inspired his more than 30 million social media followers to give away more than 20 million dollars to help some of the people and businesses featured by HONY. By highlighting the normalcy, heartbreak, hurt, kindness, and other shared human experiences, he has created what *New York Magazine* has dubbed an "Empire of Empathy."[60]

Stanton didn't start his project with a mission to create an empire of any kind. Nor did he imagine, as a young artist, that he would ever become a fundraiser who has helped change lives and save businesses. He started with a personal goal that morphed as he grew personally and saw opportunities for greater impact. Those opportunities weren't created solely by him. They came about through connection—through the community he'd created. Sure, viral posts helped, but even those posts are a lesson in connection. They are passed from

---

[59] "Humans": Connecting with the world one photo at a time. *CBS Sunday Morning.* December 13, 2020. https://www.youtube.com/watch?v=eSUDUbk2rf4&ab_channel=CBSSundayMorning.

[60] Miller, Lisa. "Brandon Stanton's Empire of Empathy: How Humans of New York became a one-man philanthropy machine." *New York Magazine,* March 2, 2022. https://nymag.com/intelligencer/article/humans-of-new-york-brandon-stanton.html#comments.

one person to hundreds and hundreds to thousands or even millions.

It all started, though, with one person connecting with another.

Brandon took action on an idea, and doing so changed his life.

Just know that whatever idea you want to see come to life starts with you.

Who's in Your Network?

The secret to success in life and in business is learning how to connect and form relationships with other people—and most people don't know how to do that.

—Joe Polish, What's in It for Them?

To be successful in almost any endeavor, you're going to need people. That's true for everyone. We all need people to educate, encourage, invite, buy from, sell to, mentor, work with, work for, help, and follow us.

You need those connections. In other words, you need a network.

If the thought of networking makes you cringe, I get it. I've been to those events where people shove their business cards into your hand, give you their thirty-second pitch, and then move on to their next victim without bothering to ask your name. It's like speed dating for business owners and just as unpleasant.

The equivalent digital approach is the random invitations to connect on LinkedIn when you know that 1) the person only wants your money, or 2) the person doesn't care about you but wants to connect with one of your connections. The random followers on Instagram who are there to boost their numbers or scam you are even worse.

That's not networking.

That's not even really meeting people.

And it certainly isn't connecting.

Author, marketer, and Founder of Genius Network Joe Polish has been called the most connected man on the planet, and for good reason: He seems to know everyone, and if he doesn't know someone yet, he knows someone who does. Networking hasn't just built his career—it *is* his career—so you can imagine that he takes it seriously.

Polish explains, "Connecting with people requires a balance of trust, rapport, and comfort."[61] Not coincidentally, the title of his latest book is *What's in It for Them?* It's a question that drives his interactions and is what makes people *want* to connect with him. This first approach to others that looks to be useful rather than to simply be served establishes those three key elements of trust, rapport, and comfort.

Trust comes from authentic interactions, being true to who you are while taking the time to get to know the other person.

You build **rapport** by investing time and energy in the relationship. This happens when you look for ways to help them or meet their needs, encourage them by validating their character, skills, or accomplishments, and are curious enough to ask them questions about themselves.

With those two elements in place, people will develop a level of **comfort** with you. They will be more likely to engage fully in the relationship. That engagement could be anything from becoming a customer to referring you to their friends

---

[61] Polish, Joe. *What's in It for Them?* Hay House: Carlsbad, California. 2022

or colleagues or connecting you with someone who can help you or your business grow.

Sometimes, this process happens slowly. It can take a few days, weeks, or months to establish a strong relationship with some people. Even if they immediately like you, proximity and limited opportunities for interaction can slow things down.

Or, as Brandon Stanton has shown with his work, powerful connections can happen in a matter of minutes. It doesn't take hours for Stanton to convince people to talk with him and allow him to take their portraits, but it does take trust, rapport, and comfort. He builds trust by being intentionally polite and non-threatening when he approaches someone to request to take their photo. Rapport develops as he asks safe and simple questions to get to know the person. When Stanton understands what's important to people, he asks deeper or more personal questions and listens to their answers. The more he asks and listens, the more comfortable people feel talking to him. So comfortable, in fact, that they often seem to forget that their picture and story will be posted for more than 30 million people to see and read. Without taking the time to establish trust, build rapport, and create a level of comfort, Stanton's *Humans of New York* would never have become known worldwide. He needs people to photograph and stories to tell. He needs people to succeed.

So do you.

HAVE A BIG PROBLEM TO SOLVE? DON'T JUST NETWORK. BUILD A GENIUS NETWORK.

Connecting with people is a great place to start building your network. I'm sure, in fact, that you already have some sort of network. The people you work with or for currently are part of our network. Unless you have burned your bridges, past employees, employers, clients, and coworkers are too. You're connected to people on social media and through your alma mater, church, civic, or interest groups. And you may even have access to *their* connections if you've begun to build trust, rapport, and comfort.

What Joe Polish calls a Genius Network˚ is about connecting with a purpose in mind. "The main difference is a Genius Network˚ is much more *intentional,* with people who come together to solve *specific* problems with the shared intention of *giving* to one another rather than simply taking," he explains. Additionally, the people in your Genius Network˚ are each well-connected and successful at some level. "The idea of Genius Network isn't something that just falls into your lap. It's about *becoming* a Genius Networker who *does* Genius Networking so they can eventually *have* a Genius Network."

So, how do you go about building a Genius Network of your own? Try this exercise from *What's in It for Them?*:

1. Draw a circle in the center of a piece of paper. This circle represents you.

2. Draw eight circles in a ring around the center circle. Write the names of the most important people in your life in each of the eight circles (one name per circle).

3. Under each name, list out that person's skills and capabilities.

4. Now, think about what each person wants or needs and how you can help those people. Then, think about how they can help you.

"As this exercise shows, Genius Networking starts with being thoughtful and learning how to be valuable to the people around you. After that, it's about connecting and spreading that value across the network—and finally, it's about using that network to solve problems. The right Genius Network is always the best tool for solutions."[62]

Great networking is never one-sided. It doesn't feel like a hit-and-run.

Great networkers always seek to help, provide value, or be useful to other people *first*.

IT'S NOT (JUST) BUSINESS. IT'S PERSONAL.

If you want to go fast, go alone. If you want to go far, go together.

—African Proverb

There's truth to the axiom *your network is your net worth.* When you have a strong network, it opens doors to business and career opportunities. You'll find people who can help you improve your financial investments or are willing to donate to a cause that changes others' lives.

Connection matters. That's true on a large scale and on a personal level. For instance, people in committed relationships tend to fare better financially. One study found that partnered adults, whether they are dating, cohabiting, or married, earn more money than their single counterparts. We know that correlation does not necessarily mean causation, but you can't help but notice that 73 percent of men without a partner were employed, compared with 91 percent of partnered men.[63]

[62] Polish, Joe. *What's in It for Them?* Hay House: Carlsbad, California. 2022.

[63] Fry, Richard and Kim Parker. "Rising Share of U.S. Adults Are Living Without a Spouse or Partner." Pew Research. October 5,

That's a pretty significant gap between the *ares* and the *are-nots*. Maybe it's because we feel a sense of responsibility to provide for the people we care about most.

But there is so much more than money involved when we're talking about connections and networks that are built on real relationships. Positive social connections add value to every area of life and can even help you live a longer, healthier, happier life.

> POSITIVE SOCIAL CONNECTIONS ADD VALUE TO EVERY AREA OF LIFE AND CAN EVEN HELP YOU LIVE A LONGER, HEALTHIER, HAPPIER LIFE.

RELATIONSHIPS AND YOUR HEALTH

What was the first thing you did when the stay-at-home orders were lifted in your area? Did you take a vacation that the pandemic had forced you to put off? Get together with your extended family? Dine at your favorite restaurant? Whatever it was, it probably involved people—seeing them without a screen between you, maybe even shaking hands with them, or (Gasp!) hugging someone you'd missed.

When what started as a couple of weeks turned into a couple of years of social isolation, the impact of relationships on our health became more evident than ever before. It's something researchers have been studying for decades, but suddenly stats, like those below felt relevant, even personal:

- A review of 148 studies (with more than 300,000 participants) found that a people's overall survival rate increases by 50 percent when they have strong

2021. https://www.pewresearch.org/social-trends/2021/10/05/rising-share-of-u-s-adults-are-living-without-a-spouse-or-partner.

social relationships, regardless of age, sex, and initial health status."[64]

- Studies show that spending time with close friends or even people who are familiar can lower cortisol during stressful times.[65]

- Among people with existing health conditions, such as coronary artery disease, those who are socially isolated have a risk of cardiac death 2.4 times greater than their more socially connected peers.[66]

- Getting together regularly and often with people who share common interests and support positive behaviors can reduce your mortality risks, including cardiovascular, weight issues, and stress, by as much as 55 percent. Look for groups that participate in or encourage activities that contribute to this statistic:

- Physical and mental activities, such as meditation or movement, help reduce stress and its effects on the body.

[64] Doron, Tzvi. "Friends and longevity: the science of social connection." Ro.com. April 8, 2020. https://ro.co/health-guide/friends-and-longevity/#:~:text=Your%20overall%20survival%20rate%20increases,club%20is%20regular%20social%20engagement.
[65] Rodrigues, Michelle A., Si On Yoon, Kathryn B. H. Clancy, and Elizabeth A. L. Stine-Morrow (2021) "What are friends for? The impact of friendship on communicative efficiency and cortisol response during collaborative problem solving among younger and older women." *Journal of Women & Aging*, 33:4, 411-427. 2021. DOI: 10.1080/08952841.2021.1915686.
[66] Brummett Beverly H, John Barefoot John C, et all. "Characteristics of Socially Isolated Patients with Coronary Artery Disease Who Are at Elevated Risk for Mortality." *Psychosomatic Medicine.* 2001;63:267–72. https://pubmed.ncbi.nlm.nih.gov/11292274/

- Altruism and compassion contribute to better mental and emotional health, which affects physical well-being.

- Gathering with a common purpose and having a commitment to something larger than oneself creates a sense of inter-connectedness that contributes to better mental health.

- Positive social relationships may reduce substance abuse and other unhealthy lifestyle choices.[67]

People with strong social support (not just being around people but really feeling connected to others) often enjoy an indirect but positive effect on health through enhanced mental health that comes from lower stress levels and having a sense of meaning and purpose in life.[68] This is true from childhood and adolescence through old age.[69]

Dan Buettner, author of *Blue Zones*, found that quality relationships are one of the nine contributing factors to longevity (living to be 100+). Unfortunately, those relationships seem to be in short supply in the United States. In a 2013 TED-Ed presentation, Buettner noted: "Fifteen years ago, the average American had three good friends. We're down to

[67] Bruce, Marino A., David Martins, et all. "Church attendance, allostatic load and mortality in middle aged adults." *PLOS ONE.* May 16, 2017. https://journals.plos.org/plosone/article?id=10.1371/journal.pone.0177618#pone-0177618-g002

[68] Cohen Sheldon. "Social Relationships and Health." *American Psychologist.* November 2004;59:676–84. https://psycnet.apa.org/doiLanding?doi=10.1037%2F0003-066X.59.8.67.

[69] Umberson, Debra and Jennifer Karas Montez. "Social Relationships and Health: A Flashpoint for Health Policy." *Journal of Health and Social Behavior,* Vol. 51, Issue 1. October 8, 2010. https://www.ncbi.nlm.nih.gov/pmc/articles/PMC3150158/

one and a half."[70] And it seems life has only gotten lonelier. A 2019 survey found that 22 percent of Millennials have *no* friends outside family members and their partners. Among Gen Xers, 22 percent have no close friends. And 25 percent of Baby Boomers say they have no one they call a best friend.[71] Zero. If isolation kills, far too many people are at risk.

In Blue Zones around the world, geographic areas where people live the longest while enjoying good mental and physical health, community is baked into the culture. In Okinawa, Japan, for example, a centuries-old tradition assigns children to small groups called *moai*. This group becomes a second family for the child. The members of a *moai* grow up together and make a commitment to share life with one another. About half of the country's population still participate in and benefit from the social connection provided by what began as a means to ensure financial support for individuals and the community's needs. "Each member knows that her friends count on her as much as she counts on her friends. If you get sick or a spouse dies or if you run out of money, we know someone will step in and help. It's much easier to go through life knowing there is a safety net," a seventy-seven-year-old Okinawan woman explained to Buettner.[72]

[70] Buettner, Dan. "How to live to be 100+ - Dan Buettner." TED-Ed. April 17, 2013. https://www.youtube.com/watch?v=ff40YiMmVkU&t=13s&ab_channel=TED-Ed.
[71] Ballard, Jamie. "Millennials are the loneliest generation." *YouGov.co*m, July 30, 2019. https://today.yougov.com/topics/society/articles-reports/2019/07/30/loneliness-friendship-new-friends-poll-survey.
[72] Kotifani, Aislinn. Moai—This Tradition is Why Okinawan People Live Longer, Better. *BlueZones.com*. https://www.bluezones.com/2018/08/moai-this-tradition-is-why-okinawan-people-live-longer-better/.

RELATIONSHIPS AND HAPPINESS

In addition to physical health and a sense of security, strong connections can add to your overall happiness. That is, of course, as long as the relationships are positive. A comprehensive Harvard study that followed people for almost eighty years revealed that close relationships were the greatest contributor to happiness throughout the participants' lives. "Those ties protect people from life's discontents, help to delay mental and physical decline, and are better predictors of long and happy lives than social class, IQ, or even genes."[73]

The key to the benefits of close relationships is the quality of that relationship. A tenuous or contentious relationship with your parents, siblings, colleagues, spouse, or significant other can have the opposite effect. Sometimes, you have the power to influence and improve those relationships (which we'll get to in the next section). Remember, however, that it takes two to tango. It may be better, in some cases, to step away from a relationship than to subject yourself to constant frustration or pain.

RELATIONSHIPS AND PERSONAL OR PROFESSIONAL ACHIEVEMENT

As discussed in the previous chapter, a lack of discipline can stand as a roadblock between you and where you want to go—or who you want to become. Sometimes, however, try as you may, finding the discipline to persist isn't as simple as pulling yourself up by your bootstraps. If obstacles pop up continually and you find it almost impossible to stay on

---

[73] Mieno, Liz. "Good genes are nice, but joy is better." *The Harvard Gazette*. April 11, 2017.

track, it may be time to find a person or an entire network for additional support.

Accountability is a powerful discipline builder. Alcoholics Anonymous, Weight Watchers International, writing groups, and running clubs all provide accountability to keep people on track to achieve desired outcomes. Side note: Accountability is one reason group therapy can be effective. People talk openly about their pain, struggles, and hopes for the future. At the same time, that mutual vulnerability and shared focus create the trust, rapport, and comfort that establishes meaningful connections.

A business coach, financial consultant, physical trainer, or life coach can provide one-on-one guidance, accountability to stay on track, and encouragement and redirection when you fail to meet a goal or deadline. Sometimes it just takes checking in regularly with a friend or colleague to keep you focused on your objective. Knowing you need to have *something* to share the next time you meet may push you to get it done.

Entrepreneurial groups, like Joe Polish's Genius Network®, Dan Sullivan's Strategic Coach programs, and Entrepreneurs' Organization (EO), are focused on supporting and connecting business owners. Organizations like these provide training on relevant topics and often encourage collaboration among members. Some coaching programs come with a hefty entrance fee, but participants who double, triple, or 10x their revenue and profit often say the return is worth the investment.

Relationships based on common interests or goals work because, as Jon Levy, author of *You're Invited,* explains, habits, behaviors, and emotions are contagious. These groups use that truth for good, pushing everyone toward optimal outcomes.

"Our results are amplified when our relationships share a sense of community," he says.[74]

HOW: INVEST IN YOUR RELATIONSHIPS

The people around you define your success (whatever that means for you) and they have the potential to change the course of your life.

—*Jon Levy,* You're Invited

"Connecting, building trust, and being part of a community aren't just about increasing your success or health or pushing a social cause; they are about improving everyone's life in the process," writes Jon Levy in *You're Invited.* Over the past decade, Levy has done exactly that by connecting leaders from almost every industry. In his late twenties, he had the idea to invite high-profile guests to his home for dinner. At the time, he admits, he wasn't living up to his potential—and it showed in his life and lifestyle. Something had to change. So he invited twelve people he admired to dinner. He chose people he could learn from, but he also wanted them to be able to learn from and help each other—and eventually to influence the industries they represented.

Part of the uniqueness of the dinner experience is that he asks his guests to do the cooking (and the cleanup), and they aren't allowed to share their names or talk about their careers until they're sitting down for the meal. The exclusive dinner parties were a success and have become known as the Influencers Dinner. The idea has expanded in the past decade to include other events, but the purpose of building a powerful, highly influential community remains the same.

---

[74] Levy, Jon. *You're Invited.* Harper Business: New York, 2021.

CONNECT WITH THE RIGHT PEOPLE

"One of the most important things we can do is curate the people around us," Levy said in a TED Talk.[75] The intentionality that the word *curating* brings to mind may not be something you've considered before when it comes to your relationships. When you consider the impact relationships—both the good and bad—have on your health, happiness, and success, being intentional makes sense.

Joe Polish sorts businesses into two basic categories: ELF and HALF. ELF stands for *easy, lucrative,* and *fun.* HALF stands for *hard, annoying, lame,* and *frustrating.* If you also think of relationships in those terms, it's easy to decide which relationships you want to add to your collection (if we're keeping with the idea of curating) and which ones may not be worth the care and upkeep they're costing you.

INVEST TIME AND ENERGY INTO YOUR RELATIONSHIPS—AND HAVE A LITTLE FUN

"Establishing a connection is great, but good relationships are also about *growth*," says Polish. "After you've planted a seed of time, attention, money, effort, and energy, you can't just walk away. To see it grow into a tall tree with a thick trunk, you need to keep watering and tending to it.[76]

It takes time to establish relationships—the closer the relationship, the longer it takes to develop. One study found that a casual relationship might only need thirty hours to gel. It can take two to three hundred hours of interaction over the

---

[75] Levy, Jon. "Jon Levy: What makes us influential? | TED Talk." https://www.ted.com/talks/jon_levy_what_makes_us_influential

[76] Polish, Joe. *What's in It for Them?* Hay House: Carlsbad, California. 2022.

span of three or four months to develop a deep friendship.[77] But we know from personal experience that spending time with people isn't what builds connection. (If it were, everyone would look forward to holiday dinners with the family and spending more time at the office with coworkers.) Likewise, access doesn't equate to connection. Just because you run in the same circles with others doesn't mean you're automatically connected.

Connection grows as you spend time with someone, expend some kind of emotional energy, and experience a mutual vulnerability on some level. And a little fun never hurts. Researcher Jeffery Hall, the author of the study, which followed 355 adults who had relocated in the previous six months along with 112 college freshmen, found that laughing and just having fun together can enhance the bonds of friendship. "When you spend time joking around, having meaningful conversations, catching up with one another, all of these types of communication episodes contribute to speedier friendship development," Hall says.[78] The Influencers Dinners prove this point. It's the novelty of cooking and eating with strangers, Levy says, that made the dinners effective for cultivating relationships that have grown into friendships and collaborative ventures.

The question is, who's on your invitation list?

---

[77] Hall, Jeffrey A. "How many hours does it take to make a friend?" *Journal of Social and Personal Relationships.* Volume 36, Issue 4. https://doi.org/10.1177/026540751876122

[78] Denworth, Lydia. "This Is Exactly How Many Hours It Takes To Create A Lasting Friendship. *MindBodyGreen.com.* February 27, 2020. https://www.mindbodygreen.com/articles/exactly-how-many-hours-it-takes-to-create-lasting-friendship.

LISTEN.

Most people think the opposite of listening is talking when, in fact, the opposite of listening is waiting for the other person to stop talking so they can jump in and say what *they* want to say. If you want to connect deeply with someone, you have to listen. I mean, *really* listen. Pay attention to what's being said through the other person's words, tone, and body language. Listen more than you speak—without interrupting or tuning out.

When you actively listen, people open up—and that's how opportunities to expand your mutual networks, careers, or businesses, and lives come to light. "For anybody who is prioritizing what they need to say next over learning about someone else, that's where you need to flip the script," says Megan Roudebush, a networking expert and the creator of KeepWith.com, an app that teaches people how to network and keep up with connections. "Focus on, by asking questions and showing authentic interest in others, how we can build stronger relationships versus this is what I have to say next."[79]

BE AUTHENTIC.

Being authentic is, of course, being yourself—not trying to be someone else. That can include the way you build relationships. If you love meeting new people at conferences and networking events and are fueled by large crowds, pull out your business cards or QR code and go for it.

If you are less outgoing or have developed isolationist tendencies during the COVID-19 pandemic, then maybe small groups or one-on-one connecting is a better fit for you.

---

[79] "EP 344: Be A Better Networker with Megan Roudebush," Brand Builders Group, January 3, 2023, https://brandbuildersgroup.com/podcast/ep-344-be-a-better-networker-with-megan-roudebush/.

Do what works for you. If that's inviting two people to lunch, great. If it's going for a walk with someone or playing tennis, do that. Levy's Influencers Dinners are just twelve guests at a time. Somewhere between six and fifteen people is optimal for small groups that meet regularly, like a dinner club or book discussion. Even if a couple of people can't make it to a meeting, you'll still have a decent number of people to add to the conversations. Some research indicates that groups of three to five may be optimal for conversations. Any more than that, and people tend to break off on separate thought trains. Brandon Stanton says he intentionally looks for people who are alone when he's looking for a Humans of New York subject. He's learned that when people are with friends, they are more guarded about what they say about themselves.

The point: There's not *one* way to increase your network. Be authentic no matter how you choose to connect.

- **With whom do you want or need to connect?** If you've played "6 Degrees of Kevin Bacon," you've seen how one connection leads to another. You've probably seen the same thing on LinkedIn. You are only a few degrees of separation away from connecting with your next customer, business collaborator, or new best friend. If you're doing the work of building trust, rapport, and comfort with the people in your life, who knows how wide your network can expand!

- **How can you be useful to others?** You know what your superpower is, so how can you use it to help the people in your network get what they want? As Zig Ziglar taught us, "You can have everything in life you want if you will just help other people get what they want."

- **Who needs an introduction?** You can create community by connecting others, and by connecting others, you can increase your influence, your network, and your net worth. Who in your life needs to meet? Make the introduction.

7

YOU ALWAYS HAD THE POWER

The opportunity of a lifetime is to pick yourself. Quit waiting to get picked; quit waiting for someone to give you permission; quit waiting for someone to say you are officially qualified . . . and pick yourself.

—Seth Godin

"It's okay for it to be your turn."
I'd been recounting a childhood memory when my high school counselor spoke those words. The memory was of me, standing at the counter at the local Baskin Robbins, waiting to be noticed. As a short six-year-old, I was either out of the server's line of sight or just didn't look like a viable customer. I stood there waiting and watching as one tall person after another took their cones and moved on down the line to the cashier.

I am a pretty patient person, and even at six years old, I didn't mind waiting my turn. But that particular day, as I shared a memory that had, at that point, stuck with me for ten years, something must have been going on that had worn my patience thin.

My counselor's words reminded me that being patient doesn't have to equate to being passed over. Nor does taking my turn equate to steamrolling over others. (Maybe that truth is where Nancy Reagan got the title for her biography, *My Turn*.)

We all occasionally need reminders—of the fact that, as Seth Godin says, it's okay to pick ourselves. It's okay to take our turn. It's good and right to be the person we want to be—fully authentic in the best way possible.

There's a scene from *The Wizard of Oz* that I've always loved for that very reason.

It comes at the end of the movie after Dorothy and her misfit gang have finally made it to the Emerald City, only to discover that the wizard—the one who was supposed to have all the answers—wasn't what they expected or hoped.

(I'm assuming you've seen the movie, but if not, spoiler alert: This film was released in 1939, so I don't feel too badly about letting the cat—or lion—out of the bag.)

The wizard, by his own admission, was a very bad wizard. He didn't possess magical powers and failed miserably at getting Dorothy home. The one thing he excelled at was the art of getting others to believe in themselves.

In response to Scarecrow's request for a brain, the wizard hands the hay-stuffed creature an honorary doctorate of *thinkology* and tells him he has all the brains he needs. Suddenly, Scarecrow has a wealth of knowledge. And why not? As the wizard explained, "Why, anybody can have a brain! That's a very mediocre commodity." In other words, everyone—even Scarecrow—is born with one. *Using* it is the issue.

The Cowardly Lion, who was afraid of everything and everyone (even himself), thought he needed courage. The wizard disagreed and awarded the lion a medal. With that and a few words acknowledging the ways Lion had previously demonstrated bravery, the big cat's fear melted away.

The Tin Man, who lacked a heart, was brave enough to want one even though he knew it could be broken. To affirm Tin Man's existing ability to love and be loved, the wizard gave him a heart pendant complete with a clock (so he had a real *ticker*).

Simply by pointing out something that was *already* true about each of them, the wizard convinced Tin Man, Lion, and Scarecrow that they possessed what they wanted most.

All they really needed was to see their true potential and believe in themselves.

(Are you seeing a pattern?)

As for Dorothy, the wizard convinces her that she needs him to get home. And that's when things go south for her. Because she believes she's dependent on someone else, her hope is crushed when the wizard accidentally leaves Oz without her.

(Have you ever been disappointed by a person or program that didn't live up to your expectations?)

Thankfully, Glenda the Good Witch floats to the rescue in her pink Technicolor bubble. Once again, a simple reminder of the truth changes everything: "You don't need to be helped any longer." Glenda says. "You've always had the power to go back to Kansas."

Dorothy finally understands. Her big *ah-ha* moment is so simple: What she wanted most was never *out there*. It was always as close as her own backyard. It was right there all along.

It isn't enough to *want* to change your life, yourself, or your circumstances.

You have to *believe* that you have the power to create that change. Because if you, like Dorothy, are expecting someone or something else to wave a magic wand and *fix* you, your life will be filled with disappointment.

That power is within you right now. Leo Tolstoy put it this way in his book by the same name: "The kingdom of God is within you."[80] You have what you need. Your heart's desire and the power to attain it lie within you. And like Dorothy, Scarecrow, Lion, and Tin Man, you have to learn that for yourself to become the *best* version of *you*.

YOU ARE THE SECRET

You never know how strong you are until being strong is the only choice you have.

—Bob Marley

You know what it takes to succeed.

It isn't a mystery.

It's not a secret that you have to go out and find.

The power to succeed lies within *you,* so stop looking outside yourself for the solution or the answer. The secret is that *you* are the secret to your success.

I know that idea seems hard to believe. After all, if you (and everyone else, by the way) already have what it takes to succeed, why are there so many courses, programs, coaches, and masterclasses out there promising to give you the answers?

One simple reason is it's profitable—for the creator, yes, but also for you. Personal development junkies love to read and learn and consume new ideas. And you know what? That's okay. Learning is good. Reading and listening to people who have done what you want to do and have gone where you want to go may be the thing that inspires you to take the

---

[80] Tolstoy, Leo. *The Kingdom of God Is Within You.* 1884.

steps you need to take to move your life in the direction you want to go.

Inspiration is powerful. Its effects are both necessary and impermanent. As Zig Ziglar commented, "People often say that motivation doesn't last. Well, neither does bathing; that's why we recommend it daily."

Inspiration only lasts so long when you're facing constant challenges. Self-doubts can slow you down. Others' negativity can stall your progress. Things you think of as failures can throw you *way* off course. Regular reminders of your capability, your innate self-worth, and your ability to learn and grow from mistakes are often just what you'll need so that you can pick yourself up, dust yourself off, and get moving again.

But I hope you're paying attention to the details here:

You are the one who picks yourself up.

You are the one who takes the next step. No one, not even six-foot-seven-inch Tony Robbins, can take those steps for you.

Read, listen, and learn. Invest in yourself.

But don't stop there. If you do, that content will only ever be profitable for the author, coach, or publisher. To make what you've learned profitable for *you*, you have to put it into action.

IT'S YOUR CHOICE

If you don't make the choices in your own life, then someone else is going to end up making them for you and they are not gonna be good.

—James Altucher

My primary goal with this book is that you close it feeling empowered and knowing that you are the author of your fate. You are not at the mercy of your current circumstances, the government, or anyone out there. You are the architect of your life.

YOU ARE NOT AT THE MERCY OF YOUR CURRENT CIRCUMSTANCES, THE GOVERNMENT, OR ANYONE OUT THERE. YOU ARE THE ARCHITECT OF YOUR LIFE.

You get to choose how you will live. No one can make that choice for you.

Waiting for the right circumstances, for the perfect conditions, or until you feel ready is like driving with your parking brake on. You might move forward, but you won't get anywhere very fast. Because you're still reading this book, I know that you're at least a little like me in that you are ready to get into gear.

You are the one with the power. Release the brake!

Choose to make the most of your talents and skills.
Choose to take consistent action.
Choose to focus on what is true and on what matters most.
Choose to accept personal responsibility for your growth.
Choose to discipline yourself to follow through.
Choose to live authentically.
Choose to become better day by day.
Choose to show yourself compassion and treat yourself with respect.
Choose to connect with yourself and others in meaningful ways.
Choose to believe in yourself.

As simple as that sounds, it isn't always easy. If it were easy, everyone would do it.
But it is possible. And you *can* do it.
And it starts with a choice.

How: Just Do It.

> *Enough words have been exchanged;*
> *now at last let me see some deeds!*

> *—Goethe, Faust I*

Nobody does anything until they *want* to do it.

That was certainly true for me. I collected the experts' secrets for years. The idea of what I wanted and who I wanted to be kept growing, but imposter syndrome and self-doubt regularly poked holes in those dreams.

It wasn't until I decided that what I wanted was worth the time, energy, and effort that I took the first step—and the next step—to make it happen.

There is one you, but there are many paths to you. Understanding the truth that *you* are the secret may mean this is the last personal development book you ever choose to read. Or this book may lead you to the path or program that makes the most sense for you. You may choose to learn from and implement tools, programs, and ideas from some of the experts I've introduced in these pages. Or you may discover new resources and people whose ideas resonate clearly with you. The point of self-help, as Mark Manson, author of *The Subtle Art of Not Giving a Fu*k,* notes, is to not need it anymore. So just remember, those tools and people aren't the answer. They are there to help you ask the right questions.

I've gained much through the years by reading and listening to people who have discovered that they were the secret to their success. Those programs, though valuable, were not the secret. They couldn't make me who I wanted to be. Only I could do that.

The same is true for you.

Stop waiting for someone or something else to give you the answer. You know what you need to do. You know who you want to be.

Put what you've learned into action and make it happen.

Do it. Now. That's what it takes to be the person you are capable of becoming.

Just. Do. It.

Pick yourself.

If I can do it, I know you can too.

You've got this!

NOTES

ABOUT THE AUTHOR

 **David Allred** is a serial entre-
preneur and lifelong student of
personal development. His varied
career has spanned from financial advisor to deputy sheriff and
a real estate broker, co-founder
of several businesses, and play
producer. From investments to
justice to homes, employees, and
thriving businesses, the common
thread is David's focus on empowering people to get what they
want or need to succeed. His current ventures include Dry
Farm Wines (DryFarmWines.com), a wine club that delivers
natural, organic wines to doorsteps across the United States,
and Zero Hunger Water (ZeroHungerWater.com), which offers
a new kind of hydration that helps curb cravings.

David splits his time between his homes in Florida and
Provence, France, where he enjoys spending time with friends
over good food and, of course, excellent wine.

Connect with David on Instagram @ David.S.Allred

Made in the USA
Middletown, DE
09 September 2024

60604546R00080